COUNTRY LIVING

SIMPLE COUNTRY WISDOM

COUNTRY LIVING
SIMPLE COUNTRY WISDOM

501 OLD-FASHIONED IDEAS
TO SIMPLIFY YOUR LIFE

SUSAN WAGGONER

HEARST BOOKS
A division of Sterling Publishing Co., Inc.

New York / London
www.sterlingpublishing.com

Copyright © 2009 by Hearst Communications, Inc.

Every effort has been made to ensure that all the information in this book is accurate. However, due to differing conditions, tools, and individual skills, the publisher cannot be responsible for any injuries, losses, and/or other damages that may result from the use of the information in this book.

Library of Congress Cataloging-in-Publication Data
Waggoner, Susan.
Country living : simple country wisdom / Susan Waggoner.
  p. cm.
Includes index.
ISBN 978-1-58816-750-7
1. Home economics. I. Country living (New York, N.Y.) II. Title.
TX158.W343 2008
640—dc22
    2008018776

10 9 8 7 6 5 4 3 2 1

Published by Hearst Books
A Division of Sterling Publishing Co., Inc.
387 Park Avenue South, New York, NY 10016

Country Living and Hearst Books are trademarks of Hearst Communications, Inc.
www.countryliving.com

For information about custom editions, special sales, premium and corporate purchases, please contact Sterling Special Sales Department at 800-805-5489 or specialsales@sterlingpublishing.com.

Distributed in Canada by Sterling Publishing
c/o Canadian Manda Group, 165 Dufferin Street
Toronto, Ontario, Canada M6K 3H6

Distributed in Australia by Capricorn Link (Australia) Pty. Ltd.
P.O. Box 704, Windsor, NSW 2756 Australia

Design: Anna Christian

Manufactured in China

Sterling ISBN 978-1-58816-750-7

CONTENTS

FOREWORD

The opening words of Leo Tolstoy's *Anna Karenina* strike an instant response in the heart of almost every reader: "Happy families are all alike; every unhappy family is unhappy in its own way." We think not only of families we have known but of houses and homes themselves. A home is more than a collection of fabric and furniture, of rooms and walls and objects. It is a thing in itself, with a personality of its own and an aura that both reflects and influences all who come its way. Tolstoy might just as well have written, "Happy homes are all alike; every unhappy home is unhappy in its own way," for that is how it seems to us.

As you can imagine, we spend a good deal of time seeing, thinking about, and knowing what makes a home special—the kind of homes we'd like to spend more time in, the kind of homes we like enough to invite *Country Living* readers into. Unhappy homes are like patients in a doctor's waiting room, some with obvious ailments—clutter or neglect—and some with disturbances less obvious, like the home that looks just fine but is so aggressively orderly there's no space left for living. Happy homes, like Tolstoy's happy families, all have a wonderful familiarity to them. They hum with energy and efficiency. They are not at war with those who live there, with a million tasks waiting at every turn, but glow with the promise of comfort and respite.

How to achieve this just-right harmony could be the study of a lifetime, for it isn't just a matter of having clean fresh sheets or an inviting guest room—it's a matter of knowing how to have them with as little fuss and waste as possible, so you can spend the precious resource of time with your friends and family, and enjoy the art of living in a home that's in harmony with itself and its environment. Author Susan Waggoner, self-described student of old ways as well as new, has gathered the best of her knowledge to share here. Whether it's a no-scrub trick to make bathroom faucets gleam, creating a garden guaranteed to attract birds and butterflies, or simple no-cost ways to slash energy consumption, her tips will help us all to live in homes that are more efficient and less demanding, with less clutter and more room for all that's joyous in life.

The editors of *Country Living*

THE HOME THAT WELCOMES

What Makes a Welcoming Home?

Where and how we live, what we do there, and how we embrace the space we're given, is surely one of the world's great themes. The *Iliad* may be about war, but the far greater *Odyssey* is about men who want nothing more than to get back to their wives, children, and vineyards. By the time she reaches the end of the Yellow Brick Road, Dorothy has no qualms at all about returning to a farm in Kansas. *The Wind in the Willows'* Mole, enticed to set off on a wild adventure, begins to long for "that little curtained world" left behind.

Most of us have a home like this somewhere in our hearts. It's the home we try to create every day. Some days we do a good job of it, some days we fall behind. Often, there's a looming sense that we should be doing something—or doing more—than we are, but we aren't quite sure what it is.

It's a unique feature of the past few generations that many of us grew up in chore-free childhoods. Even the word "chore" has an old-fashioned ring to it. So do a few other words, like "visit," "front porch," and "gracious plenty." Yet all of these words, and the things they represent, are part of that home we strive for, whether we know it or not.

PUTTING THE
ELEMENTS
TOGETHER

Over the years, we've kept the ideal but lost much of the knowledge of what it took to get there. My mother, the first woman in her family to work outside the home, never learned to bake bread—that was the point of college, after all. My grandmother never taught me because she assumed that baking bread was something everybody knew how to do. Eventually, I learned to bake bread on my own. And years later, my mother decided that bread was something she was interested in as well. Together, through the course of many trials and errors, we cloned the Swedish rye bread my grandmother had made so effortlessly. Retrieving that one little scrap of the past filled us with a profound sense of contentment. When I think of my mother's house, that day is the one I remember.

Of course, it takes more than a loaf of bread to create a home that is gracious and comforting to those within. But sometimes, the exact qualities seem elusive. Showy luxury and stadium-sized space—the qualities we are supposed to strive for—don't seem to be the secret. The ingredients

that go into a home that embraces and welcomes aren't obvious, and they aren't exactly the same for every home. Yet over the years I've noticed that such homes have certain qualities in common; understanding them can help us restore much of what's been mislaid in the scramble and tussle of modern life. Here are those key qualities.

One of the hallmarks of a warm and inviting kitchen is providing a central focus, such as this antique island complete with barstools.

HARMONY

There are all sorts of harmony, starting with the house itself. A home that suits the neighborhood, and suits the lot it sits on, conveys a sense of neighborliness and community. I always wonder about the person who breaks up a block of vintage bungalows to erect a high-tech concrete box, or the person so determined to have his starter castle that there's scarcely a foot of space between the house and the lot's perimeter.

Go out of *your way* to establish a bit of neighborhood harmony. A cousin told me about a good friend of hers who owned a large dog. Sweet and gentle, to be sure, but a dog that size could leave quite a mess if he were to slip out of his yard. So soon after moving, the owner took her dog, Vernors, on a meet-and-greet around the neighborhood. Vernors left a business card with each neighbor asking that they please call his home if he should get out and someone would be over to clean up immediately. That was all it took, and Vernors has been a popular member of the community ever since. All most folks want to know

is that, if a problem arises, they can mention it without risking an ugly episode of porch rage.

No room should be an island.

If stepping from the living room to the kitchen is like stepping from Versailles to American farm country, and the dining room is a lesson in Danish modern, the effect is jarring and the rooms feel closed off from each other. When rooms harmonize, each seems an extension of the next, and the whole house feels more spacious and at peace with itself.

Select harmonious furniture.

Does the furniture suit the purpose of the room it's in? Or does it hinder it, like a dining table centerpiece that's too big, the drive-in sized television set in the conversation room, or the reading corner with the beautiful but impossible-to-read-by lamp?

CLEANLINESS

The world makes a lot of demands on us. There's always something that needs to be done, someone we need to make time for, an item to pick up here and another to drop off there, traffic that tests our limits, friends and coworkers caught in dramas of their own, and often, at the end of the day, any number of to-dos and should-dos that already casting their shadow over tomorrow.

Your home should be a refuge

from all that. The "shelter" in the food, clothing, and shelter equation means more than mere protection from wind and rain or a place to stow one's belongings. It also means shelter from the stresses of the greater world, a little oasis where we can relax, pursue our own interests, share time with those we love.

A home that's dirty or cluttered

can't fulfill that part of the mission. How can it, when you see new tasks waiting at every turn: the vacuum cleaner that didn't get put away, the pile of mail waiting to be sorted through, the laundry you meant to put away three days ago, the gritty, sticky corner of the kitchen floor that you meant to go at with hot water and suds but haven't quite gotten around to. And even if you put all these chores off one more day, you still feel oppressed by them, drained of energy and a little guilty. Far from being a mundane concern, learning how to keep a house clean and uncluttered is the groundwork for many loftier achievements—happiness, thriving family relationships, intellectual pursuits, hobbies that nurture creativity, and renewed energy and enthusiasm for the life we live outside the home.

Beyond a certain level of clean, I've noticed that homes that feel welcoming all have a "tended to" look. Items that need repair aren't in evidence; they've been removed to the basement or garage. Valentine's streamers aren't dangling as Easter eggs are being deviled. Most of all, someone has taken the trouble to make things nice—to fluff up the pillows, fill a vase with flowers, put down freshly laundered throw rugs, or set a pot of potpouri to simmer. These little grace notes of sight and scent do more to make a home feel gracious and expansive than all the expensive furniture in the world.

EFFICIENCY

Before you conjure images of Captain von Trapp marching his children around to the beat of a military whistle, or a time management specialist moving people from one task to another without a single pause, rest assured: that's not what we mean. Yes, it might be more efficient to set the table for breakfast as soon as dinner is finished—but then no one could play Monopoly at the kitchen table or relax over a cup of bedtime cocoa, now could they?

An efficient home is one that runs smoothly and doesn't get in the way of the people who live there. This takes some behind-the-scenes effort—planning the rooms to accommodate the needs and activities of the people who live in them, understanding what tasks need to be done and who will do them, and planning for the "when" and "how" of seeing the job through. Just as in the days of the family farm, efficiency means that everybody has a job to do, and pitches in when someone else is sick, has a test to study for, or extra responsibilities outside the home.

Those who live in gracious homes tend not to be wasteful. Furniture and possessions are treated with care and made to last. Water isn't left running and lights aren't left on, and possessions

A NEATLY ORGANIZED RIBBON AND BUTTON STATION HELPS TO MAKE WRAPPING PRESENTS AND CRAFTING PROJECTS IN UNIQUE PACKAGES A JOYFUL AND EFFICIENT TASK.

aren't acquired without thought. This means that what is used is needed, what is bought is fully enjoyed, and what's left over can be shared with others.

SELF-RELIANCE

No one can be truly self-sufficient in this day and age, and I wouldn't even try, but I'm sure that a way of life in which each of us does just one or two things and outsources all the rest won't be too rewarding, either.

Households that preserve the do-it-for-ourselves tradition seem to me happier, livelier, and more interesting places to be, and the people who live there are almost always people I want to know. You don't need to spin your own wool or make your own furniture to get in the spirit, either. Try making your own pizza instead of having it delivered, growing no-fuss vegetables like scallions and radishes, or taking on a do-it-yourself project that you're pretty sure you can do yourself. Pick up a crafting hobby like knitting, quilting, or sewing. You'll live a richer, more varied life because of it.

Fun is another kind of self-reliance that's worth bringing into your home. Turn off the DVD player, shut down the computer, and actually do something. Read a book, play charades, work a jigsaw puzzle, get out the badminton set, let the rafters ring with activity— studies show that any of these will make you happier than another night in front of a glowing screen.

GENEROSITY

We've all been in one at one time or another—a home that's the best money can buy, filled with expensive objects and furnished for royalty. There's just one problem: you can't wait to get out of the place. It's amazing how many top-flight homes have a total absence of grace and charm. They're filled with expensive antiques you're afraid to sit on, overwhelm you with enough marble to pave the courtyards of Versailles, and do everything they can to make you feel out of place.

At the other extreme is the modest home that might charm if only the owner would stop fussing over everything and everyone in it. Sigmund Freud may never have cleaned a house, but he had this one pegged. In an early case study, describing the home life of his troubled young client, he noted that household was a spacious and well-appointed one, but presided over by a mother who cleaned and polished so relentlessly that it was impossible for anyone who lived there to enjoy it.

A home has to be comfortable. Once upon a time, everyone knew that, and filled their rooms with overstuffed chairs, afghans, and padded footstools. That was before the age of overdesign. Now, all too often, the way a chair looks can trump its usability, and homeowners get carried away with the notion of staging a room to look just so.

Try sitting in every chair in the room for about half an hour. Is it comfortable? You should never keep a piece of furniture you don't like sitting in—even if it's a chair that only gets used when company comes. What kind of logic is that? While you're sitting there, you might also try reading a book or having a cup of tea. How's the lighting? Is there a place to set your teacup? Oh, that's right. You decided a lamp would spoil the room's look entirely, and no one should be drinking tea there anyway because the cup might leave a ring. While you're holding on to your teacup, evaluate the room's emotional effect. Do you feel at ease and confident, or do

YOU SHOULD NEVER KEEP A PIECE OF FURNITURE YOU DON'T LIKE SITTING IN— EVEN IF IT'S A CHAIR THAT ONLY GETS USED WHEN COMPANY COMES.

you feel that you do not fit, and perhaps someone else should be sitting in your spot?

PERSONALITY

Homes that welcome you in don't eradicate signs of life, they embrace them. They reflect the personalities and interests of the people who live there and convey a sense of life going on in all its bustling, varied, and not necessarily predictable ways.

I have a friend who's one of the liveliest, most intelligent women I know, one of those people with a dynamic personality and sparkling presence that everyone responds to. Yet the first time I visited her home, I was stunned. The rooms were tasteful and well-decorated, the furniture was comfortable and inviting, yet I was bored out of my mind. There wasn't a single scrap of my friend's personality in the room, or of her husband's or her children's. I felt I'd visited a rather nice suite in a very good hotel. When we became better friends, she told me about her collection of vintage tablecloths and kitchenware, and the daisy-strewn dishes she'd inherited from an aunt. Thinking of how much I would have enjoyed seeing these things, I asked her why she didn't put them out. She told me she thought they might "clutter up" the kitchen. I'm not so sure they would, but even if they did, I'd take some really good, interesting clutter over antiseptic, impersonal neatness any day of the week.

Putting personality in the place you live is easy—just go with your tastes and interests. If you think the Depression-era glass plates your grandmother got with cereal coupons is prettier than your sophisticated, eggshell-thin Rosenthal, go ahead, fill your shelves with the Depression glass and put the Rosenthal away. If you adore your collection of Populuxe barware, complete with pink elephants cavorting around a cocktail shaker, find a way to work it into your decor. The easy way to do this, of course, is to start out with an overall style you like rather than the trend of the moment or the style that's so neutral it doesn't even have a name. Chances are that all the things you love and have acquired over the years go together pretty well, and will work to create a home that reflects your personality. The worst question to be asked by the person who visits for the first time is, "I love this, who's your decorator?" But when you hear someone say, "This place is so you," you know you've created something special.

A collection of mismatched eggcups becomes
a quirky candleset, perfectly matching the owner's tastes.

WHAT MAKES A WELCOMING HOME?

A set of binoculars invites guests to take a seat on this quaint porch and indulge in a few moments of birdwatching.

JOY

Warm, life-filled homes have a pulse and a rhythm. They celebrate the seasons with wreaths of autumn leaves in the fall and baskets of tulips in the spring. They get dressed for the holidays and sometimes, just like their occupants, they get new haircuts and outfits and even major makeovers. Most of all, they develop traditions of their own. It may be a gesture as simple as turning on a lamp in the window for the one coming home, or popping corn and watching movies together on Friday nights. It may be rushing out to toast the first snowfall of the season with a bottle of champagne or an annual summer garage sale, held by everyone in the house, with the proceeds going into a piggy bank marked "Disney World." It matters less what the traditions are than that they exist. When we go away, this is what we remember—how things were done in that special place, and how the doing and the sharing filled us with happiness and a sense of well-being.

They say that people fall in love with houses, but houses never love you back, and I suppose that's true. But if you take time to manage your little part of the world, if you put energy and thought into the way things are done, you'll receive some things that are pretty valuable in return— comfort and joy, time to relax and appreciate your life and the people in it, and rooms that welcome you each time you return. All in all, pretty well worth the effort.

Clutter Control

The loveliest, best-planned home in the world can be completely undone by the detritus of everyday living. In our more-is-more culture, we are constantly urged to buy more, have more, act now and get one free. Clutter is so pervasive in our lives we often don't notice it. We ask ourselves how our neighbors can live with stacks of magazines or much too much furniture, then go home and don't even notice that the kitchen counter has become such a jungle of canisters, small appliances, and bottles of gourmet oils that there's barely any workspace left.

Whether we notice our clutter or not, it still takes its toll. We pay for it in time spent on extra cleaning and searching for items that aren't where they should be. We pay for it in strained relationships with the people we live with, and loss of the comfort and joy a home should bring. Often we literally pay for it, since misplaced objects tend to get broken, accidentally thrown out, or lost for years on end. A perpetually cluttered home can make you hesitate to ask guests over, or make you so self-conscious while they're there you can't enjoy the visit. Suddenly, you're seeing your home through their eyes and it isn't pretty.

THE FIRST STEP

This isn't what we had in mind when we moved in, or bought paint and furniture and invested so much time and energy in making things look just right. Yet here it is—clutter. And the more clutter there is, the more overwhelmed we feel. Instead of being a calming oasis, the house we live in becomes one giant to-do list, with a clean-up task at every turn. Before things reach critical mass, here are some ways to take control.

Cut the clutter by not bringing it into your home in the first place. Resist salvaging things your friends are tossing out, and only buy things that are on sale if you were already shopping for them.

Know where it's going to go. If you don't know exactly where it's going to go, and what you plan to do with the item currently occupying that space, don't buy it.

Be realistic about the storage space that's available in your home. Appliance garages aren't bottomless pits, and chances are

{ Filled with collected treasures, this bookshelf offers up more than just books—but still remains functional. }

that the armoire that seemed so empty a year ago has filled itself up when you weren't looking.

A good spot to start paring down is the bookshelf. Having bought thousands of books over the course of my lifetime, I've learned a few things. First, if I check a book out of the library, it will get read years sooner than if I own it, so the library is always my first choice. Second, of the 50 to 100 books I read a year, there are probably only one or two I really want to own. Everything else gets passed along to friends or donated to the library. Third, most of the reference books we think of as must-haves—dictionaries, world atlases, encyclopedias, and the like—are now available free on the Internet, along with resources like road maps, information on illness and disease, and consumer buying guides. The fun stuff is available too, from movie guides to recipes to how-tos for hobbies and crafts.

Go through your holiday decorations once every few years and throw out decorations that have grown shabby, that you no longer use, or that no longer fit with your home's decor.

Furniture that doesn't fit, no matter how wonderful, is just clutter unless it truly fits the space and style surrounding it. Rethink your room arrangement or trade it in for something better-suited to your decor.

WHEN IT'S TIME FOR A MAJOR CLEANUP, GIVE CHILDREN GUIDELINES TO WORK WITHIN, THEN LET THEM DECIDE WHICH TOYS TO KEEP AND WHICH ONES TO PASS ALONG.

Make an annual giveaway part of your schedule. Find out when the local rummage sales are, or find like-minded friends and agree to have a joint annual garage sale. Having a target date will get you moving.

Give yourself an incentive. Decide what you want to do with money from items that are sold at garage sales or on eBay. If you donate items, get a receipt—as a charitable contribution, it's tax deductible.

MAJOR CLUTTER CLEANUPS

Every home has spots that are a Sargasso Sea for clutter. Objects come to rest there and circle around in a sulky tide, but they never seem to break free and sail away. Identify the trouble spots in your home and tackle those first. Don't just pick up the clutter, but look for ways to permanently resolve the problem. For many of us, the hot spot is the kitchen table. The solution may be as simple as making a habit of clearing the table completely before every meal. Items that end up in one place over and over again may have no home of their own. Or the home they have isn't working. If the desk at which you're supposed to do your household accounts is cramped and poorly lit, chances are your account books will end up in whatever area you find more comfortable. Ask yourself what would make that forlorn little desk more appealing to you. Better lighting? A radio to keep you company? A more comfortable chair? The answer may be simpler, and far less expensive, than you think.

Make a master plan for doing a major cleanup if your home has become very cluttered. Give yourself an ample calendar to work with, set specific goals, and take on one room at a time—or one closet at a time if that's all your schedule allows.

{ Making sure each space in the house works well and serves its
intended purpose will help control clutter throughout the entire house. }

SET ASIDE TIME EACH DAY FOR
CLEARING UP CLUTTER. I LIKE
DOING IT WHILE DINNER IS COOKING,
OR JUST AFTER SUPPER. THEN I CAN
RELAX AND SPEND THE EVENING
ENJOYING MY TIDY HOME.

Get out a camera and start taking pictures. I learned this one from a photographer's stylist. Photos show you things the eye edits out, and anything that's out of place will stand out like a flashing neon sign.

Don't try to do it all yourself unless you live alone. Ask everyone in the house to be responsible for stowing their own things at the end of the day. Giving children bright plastic buckets or bins and helping them round up their toys before bed cuts your workload and encourages good habits.

Make sure everything has a place where it belongs. Items that are floaters never really get put away, just moved from room to room.

Stop object migration. Look around the room you're sitting in. How many items do you see that don't belong there? Never leave a room empty-handed—always take something with you, and return it to its rightful home.

Keep going until it's done. If you're clearing up the kitchen and find something that belongs in the bedroom, don't drop it off in the dining room. That's not clearing up, just shifting the clutter. Once something is in your hand, keep going until you've returned it to the room it really belongs in.

Invest in a large, attractive basket with a handle that you can tote things up and down your stairs in. You can let objects bound for the next level gather there, yet the basket is attractive enough to seem like part of the decor.

Wherever possible, go digital. Anything you can store or access in digital format—music, video, research, and all the rest—is a giant space-saver.

Clean the hidden stash. Remember that whirlwind cleanup job you did a few weeks ago, when you gathered all the magazines, projects, and other clutter in a shopping bag and dumped the bag in a closet—and left it there?

{
An umbrella stand
by the front door will help keep
both you and your floors dry.
}

Sometimes an emergency clean-and-stash is unavoidable. But once the company has left, finish the job the right way.

Don't alphabetize your books, CDs, or DVDs—it takes far too long to re-shelve them. Arrange by categories, and when it's time to put the items back, close enough will be good enough.

Have a system for keeping magazines from piling up. First, enjoy the pleasure of paging through the magazine and reading it. That's why you subscribed in the fist place. When the magazine is a few weeks old, go through it a second time. Tear out whatever you want to keep, stapling continued articles together. Put everything you're keeping in an office envelope and discard the rest. In a few months, sit down and go through your stack of saved stuff. Invariably you'll find that, swept up in the excitement of the moment, you saved a lot of things for reasons you can no longer remember. I can't tell you how many times I've turned a page of recipes over and over, unable to figure out which one appealed to me in the first place.

All of these mystery pages can now be discarded. Going through your stack, you'll also find articles that delight you all over again. These are the keepers, and you want to be able to find them when you need them. I keep my saved articles in folders in a file cabinet, with a folder for each major interest—reviews of books I want to read, recipes, craft ideas, home decoration, and so on. Every few years, I weed out things I'm no longer interested in, so the files stay trim and tidy as well.

WHAT NOT TO SAVE

When the clutter has accumulated and you need to do a general clearing out, here are some easy decision-makers.

Don't save something you forgot you had. If you haven't missed it yet, you probably will never miss it.

Just because it was free, you don't need to keep it. If you don't

IF YOU HAVE LOTS OF SHIRTS
AND BLOUSES IN YOUR CLOSET,
THE SPACE UNDERNEATH THEM MIGHT
BE BIG ENOUGH TO HOLD A CLOTHES
HAMPER, SOME SHELVES, OR EVEN
A SMALL CHEST OF DRAWERS.

like it well enough to have paid for it, toss it.

Don't warehouse pieces of furniture, appliances or electronics that "still have some life in them" and "somebody might need someday." Someone needs these things now, and they'll find them faster if you drop them off at the secondhand store.

It might come in handy someday, but not anytime soon. Yes, you might need package wrap and tissue paper sometimes, and your 12-year-old will definitely need sheets and towels when he goes to college, but chances are 99 to 1 that you won't be able to find the tissue paper when you need it, and your college freshman won't want your old sheets with the faded violets on them.

Toss the guilt. This includes gifts you never liked, family "heirlooms" that seem more like albatrosses, and buying mistakes you've sentenced yourself to live with. If you really want to be kind to these objects, give them a new home with people who will appreciate them. Share the heirlooms with family members who want them, and let everything else be someone else's flea market treasure.

> This armoire serves as a neatly organized and accessible linen closet in the kitchen.

ALL ABOUT CLOSETS

Closets weren't invented until fairly recently. For thousands of years, humans ran about in blissful ignorance, stowing extra skins in the back of the cave, tossing clothes in chests and trunks, keeping linens in cupboards, and leaving the broom right outside the cabin door. Then one day someone must have looked at an assortment of items his wife had just asked him to take

Lots of things don't fit conveniently, and shoes are right at the top of the list. The worst option is leaving them in a heap on the closet floor. At the very least, find a basket to contain them. If you have room on your closet shelves, storing seldom-worn pairs in their boxes is an excellent way to tame the clutter. Displaying your rainboots in the mudroom will keep you organized and serve as a reminder next time it pours.

out to the shed and thought, "If only this stuff had a little room of its own, right here in the house, I could shove it all in there and be done with it." It was a real turning point in history. Because, of course, where space exists, clutter follows. In 1900, closets barely existed. A few decades later, the jammed-to-bursting closet was the biggest laugh Fibber McGee and Molly ever got. For anyone whoever's ever been afraid to open that door, here are some tips for neater storage.

Know what's in your closets. Lots of us don't, and the deeper into the closet you go, the more you find yourself stumbling across the unknown. If this is the case, drag everything out of the closet. Anything that makes you say, "I'd forgotten all about that," should go into the discard pile. Anything that makes you say, "I've been looking all over for that," should be given a new

home, so you can find it when you need it.

Set a limit on nostalgia clothes. Save one or two of the dresses you loved, and a few of your children's outfits. Let the rest go. You had the good times, and the sweet memories will always be with you.

Be honest with yourself when deciding which clothes to keep and which to discard. Are you really going to fit into those too-tight items anytime soon? And yes, those older items will be back in style someday, but will you be in style in them? Vintage clothes only really work if they're from someone else's youth, not yours. As for the "perfectly good" pieces that you don't like and never wear—let someone else find the good in them.

If you buy a piece of clothing to replace something that's

DIVIDE AND CONQUER

When you clean a closet, try the "four piles" method:

1 **Establish four piles in the room:** Keep, Repair, Give Away, and Discard.

2 **As you take each item out of the closet,** put it in one of the piles. You must empty the closet completely, and everything must go to one of the piles. Notice that there is no "decide later" pile.

3 **When the closet is completely empty,** look at the Keep pile. If it's still bigger than you hoped, trim it by 10 percent. Repeat this step until you're satisfied with the size of the pile. Return the keepers to the closet.

4 **Now examine each item in the Repair pile.** Which ones are really worth repairing? Who's going to do the work? When will the work get done? How much will it cost, in time as well as dollars? Answer these questions honestly, and you'll probably be able to reduce this pile by 50 percent or more. Give yourself a deadline for items you plan to repair. Bundle them together in a bag or box, write the deadline date on it, and move it to your work area. On deadline day, throw away whatever hasn't been attended to.

5 **Take a second pass through the Give Away pile.** Transfer items that are shabby, stained, and badly broken to the discard pile. Bag or box the remaining items and drop them off within the next week.

6 **Bag the items in the discard pile** and carry them out to the trash. Immediately.

Think creatively when looking for storage.
An attractive way to display your pearls, hats, and purses
is by having them as part of the décor.

worn or stained, throw the old piece away as soon as you get home. If you don't, you haven't "replaced" anything, just added to a crowded closet.

I used to line my purses up on a closet shelf, but every time I pulled one down, several more came tumbling with it. Then one day I was in an office supply store and saw a world of possibilities—stackable letter trays, desktop file holders, tiered desk shelves. The dimensions were perfect for the closet, and for less than twenty dollars I solved my problem. Now each of my purses is stored in its own slot, and I can get one down without dragging the others with it.

Small clothespins—the kind you find in craft stores—are an excellent way to keep wide-necked items from sliding off the hanger. They'll also keep hangers from creating those annoying bumps in your shoulder seams.

Add extra storage to clothes closets. A narrow bookcase, turned on its side on a closet shelf, makes a series of cubbies to hold T-shirts, sweaters, shoes, and other items.

At the end of the winter, round up all the coats, scarves, mittens, and caps and decide which should be given away or discarded. Take care of any repairs that need to be done on the items you plan to use next year, have them cleaned, then put them away.

Store away scarves, caps, and mittens in hat boxes made to fit on closet shelves. If you have a choice, always choose square or rectangular boxes over round ones—you get more storage space for the room they take up.

Cedar wood blocks make excellent closet air fresheners, but all too soon the scent vanishes. Don't throw the blocks away—get out your sandpaper and give them a light sanding; the scent will come back full strength.

What Meets the Eye

Furniture, wall color, lighting, accessories, even the scent drifting in the air—beyond our home's utilitarian purpose, most of us want a home to please, comfort, and even inspire us. Most of all, we want to look around the place we live and see our own interests and tastes reflected. Yet the task of getting from point A to point B, of choosing from so many options and adding details and touches of our own, can seem overwhelming. I sometimes feel that, to get my home looking the way I want it to, I need to stop work and enroll in a design course. Fortunately, it doesn't really need to be that difficult. You have an idea of how you want your home to look. Here are some design reminders to get it that way.

CHOOSING YOUR COLORS

Paint, as almost everyone knows by now, is the quickest, easiest, and least expensive renovation tool known to man. Paint can change a room's mood and style. It can make a gloomy room seem cheerful and a small room seem large. In Colonial New England, where winters were bleak and home heating was in its infancy, bright cherry red was the wall color of choice because it made the room feel warm and fire lit. And it's no accident that in Scandinavia, where sunlight is scarce or wholly absent for many months of the year, yellow houses dot the landscape. If you love your house, or want to rekindle the romance, it's worth knowing how to use paint. Then you'll be free to change, freshen, and experiment to your heart's content.

Visit paint manufacturers' Web sites. Many have sample rooms you can "paint" with colors and contrasts to see how the shade

Tape several color swatches to the wall you're going to paint and forget about them. Whenever you walk by or happen to glance in that direction, with all the decision-making pressure off, your eye will automatically gravitate to one color again and again. That's your color.

you're contemplating would look. Computer colors aren't exact because monitors don't all display alike, but you'll get a good idea of how your shade might look in a big space.

Buy a small can of the colors you're debating between and try

DON'T BE AFRAID TO GO BOLD. MOST PEOPLE PLAY IT SAFE, AND DON'T GET THE EFFECT OR THE DRAMA THEY WERE HOPING FOR.

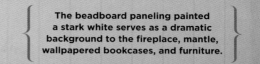
The beadboard paneling painted a stark white serves as a dramatic background to the fireplace, mantle, wallpapered bookcases, and furniture.

them. You don't need to mess up your walls to do it, either. Find some large pieces of cardboard or posterboard, give them a few coats of primer, and paint them. Thumbtack the finished masterpiece to the wall, live with it for a week or so, and you'll probably be able to make a decision.

If you want light ceilings but not white, as its prone to glaring, look at the lightest color on the sample strip. Often, it's an off-white subtly tinted with the dominant pigment. If that isn't the case, ask the paint store to make a custom tint for you. You ceiling will look white, but won't outshine your walls.

Buy metal paint trays, even though they cost more than plastic and you're going to throw them away in the end. The plastic ones crack easily and it doesn't take much to tip them over, so metal reduces the chances of a really messy accident.

Ask store personnel for advice. Most of them are very knowledgeable, can tell you the best way to accomplish what you want to do, and can keep you from getting off on the wrong foot. Finding out whether or not you need to lay down a coat of primer first is a good place to start. Painting a dark wall a lighter shade or using latex paint over an oil base requires a primer, but there are other conditions that do as well, so take the time to find out.

After painting a room, but before putting away your tools, find a piece of cardboard the size of a sheet of typing paper and paint it the color of your new room. When it's dry, write the name of the manufacturer, the paint number, and the name of the shade on it. When you go shopping for new items for the room, you have a giant-sized swatch to take with you.

> Sometimes, there's a bold color you love but just know wouldn't work in the whole room. Try painting a limited area with it—a single wall (such as this orange overhang in this cheerful bedroom), the inside of bookshelves, the wall extending above the fireplace. That jolt of color can add a bright note without overwhelming the entire room.

LIKE THE WALLPAPERED LOOK BUT DON'T WANT THE WALLPAPER? CONSIDER STENCILING. A MOTIF CAN BE REPEATED AT MEASURED INTERVALS TO GIVE THE SAME LOOK, BUT WITHOUT THE COMMITMENT.

HOW TO PAINT A ROOM

A refreshed room begins at the paint store. If it's been a while since you've painted, be sure to check out the latest gadgets. As I discovered last time I painted, edgers, extenders, pint-sized rollers, and a lot of other gear now make it possible to do perfect walls and ceilings in places that won't accommodate a ladder.

Once you're home with your paint, it's time to take everything off the walls and take everything that's moveable—including furniture—out of the room. It seems like a lot of work, but it will more than pay you back when it's time to paint.

Push all the remaining furniture to the center of the room and cover with the plastic sheets you bought at the paint store.

Cover the floor as much as possible with drop cloths. You may not be painting on the other side of the room yet but trust me, someone with paint on their shoe will be sure to walk wherever there isn't a cloth. I prefer to use old sheets that can be thrown away when I'm finished as drop cloths rather than the plastic drop cloths sold at the paint store, because the plastic slides around.

Examine the walls for cracks and divots that need spackling. If you're filling in a divot, remember that spackle shrinks as it dries, so you may need to do a second application. Be sure to let the spackle dry at least as long as the can says—longer, if possible, to make sure there's no further shrinkage or cracking.

Wash the walls with soapy water, even though you're about to paint over them. While you're at it, dust or wash the baseboards as well. Paint doesn't adhere well if the walls are dirty, and painter's tape doesn't cling to dirty woodwork. A quick version is to dust the walls lightly and thoroughly clean the baseboards.

Remove electrical outlet plates and register covers, and cover the switches and outlets with tape to guard against drips. Tape each set of screws to the plate to which they belong.

Protect the baseboards by running a strip of painter's tape along the upper edge. Press it down as you go and, instead of pressing it down to cover the baseboard, let it stick out horizontally—it will work like a tray to catch drips. Tape around the windows and door frames as well.

Work from the top down. Splatters happen, so this way you won't be splattering a wall you just painted. Start with the ceiling and crown molding. If you are painting the crown molding a different shade from the ceiling, you will need to avoid marring the freshly painted area. If you have a steady hand and a lot of confidence, use a small brush to carefully paint the edge of the molding that abuts the ceiling. Small spots and smears can be touched up later. If this idea makes you weak at the knees, there are a couple of alternatives. One is to a hold a straight-edged metal trowel against the ceiling as you paint. You can also use painter's tape, but that means waiting for the ceiling to be thoroughly dry. I've learned that "dry" and "thoroughly dry" are two different things. The ceiling may feel dry to the touch, but using tape too soon may cause damage if it isn't completely set. How long this takes depends on the humidity in your home, and how thick or thin the coat of paint was.

continued on next page

continued from previous page

> Now you're ready for the walls. Again, start at the top. Use a brush or an edging pad to paint a clean straight edge where the wall joins the ceiling or molding. Use a brush to paint the upper few inches of the wall, the corner seams, and about six inches around the windows and doors.

After you've taken care of the areas that must be done by hand, switch to your roller. Thanks to all your prep work, you'll be amazed to see how little time it takes to cover the wall.

Step back every so often to see if there are places you missed. Remember, though, that paint changes color constantly as it dries, so the piece of wall you just did won't look like the patch you started with. I've found it easier to let the whole area dry, then apply a second coat if needed.

If you've finished your paint job in one day, throw the rollers away. If you plan to paint tomorrow or the next day, wash your rollers and brushes in warm water (assuming you're using latex paint), squeeze them out, and let them dry.

My personal advice when it comes to rollers is to buy a roller cover for every day you plan to paint. It takes gallons of water to get the paint out of the roller, and mine seldom dry completely before I'm ready to paint the next day. This is a problem because the roller that feels just a little damp has a considerable amount of moisture in it, and the moisture dilutes your paint and makes for a bad paint job. So starting with a new roller cover every session is much easier, saves a lot of water, and results in a far better paint job.

When the room is dry, replace the switch plates and register covers and enjoy putting your new room back together.

I used to save all of my leftover paint, just in case. Eventually, I realized two things. First, if I ever needed to do more than a touch-up, I'd have to buy new paint and re-do the whole room anyway, because the old paint would have faded and the large touch-ups wouldn't match. I also realized that paint left in a can with a lid that no longer seals dries out, and paint taken out to the garage freezes. Now I pour enough for minor touch ups in a small mayonnaise jar and dispose of the rest.

Use a drop of paint on a cotton swab to touch up a scratch or other type of blemish on a painted wall. You won't waste a bunch of paint and you won't have to waste time cleaning a paint brush.

Keep a damp cloth with you when you're painting. Wipe up any splatters right away, and wipe your hands often to avoid accidentally leaving a trail of fingerprints where you don't want them.

{ **A small collection of mirrors brightens this white staircase.** }

DECORATING TIPS

When it comes to home décor, trends aren't necessarily your friends. It's easy to get swept up in the color or style of the moment, but the result can be a cookie-cutter look and, a few years down the line, an embarrassing abundance of peach wallpaper, shag carpeting, and avocado appliances. It's best to stick with a style you love, whether it's English cottage, mid-century modern, or farmhouse style, and leave the trend setting to others. Your personal style will always be classic for you, and the only reason you'll end up with green shag is because you love it.

Keep a folder or notebook of ideas you like, and look through it often. Over time, two things will happen. You'll keep coming back to certain looks over and over again, and they'll seem as fresh and enticing as ever. When it's time to

Bedecked with vintage lace, the antique furniture, mirrors, and china sparkle against the clean white paint palette.

{ Make a small room seem larger by choosing glass-fronted cupboards and cabinets that add visual depth. }

If you see a room you really, really love, copy it—even if everything in the photo is way out of your price range and a few don't quite match your style. With a little thought and creative shopping, you can find items that give the same look and feel, and adapt the ones that don't to better suit you.

Keep a file for your house as well, and the record of the work you've done on it. It's especially useful to note the name, number, and brand of paint you used on a room, as well as a super-sized paint chip to help you choose new fabrics and furniture that harmonize. It's also a good idea to note the manufacturer of various pieces of furniture, and keep a record and receipt of the purchase.

Invest in storage. It's easy to get carried away over lamps and chairs and yet another end table, but storage that looks good is worth its weight in gold.

remodel, you'll have a much clearer idea of what you want. In fact, you may find that, without realizing it, you've already been subtly moving in that direction in your choice of new accessories and minor upgrades, so your major remodel might not require the major effort and expenditure it otherwise would. The other thing that will happen is that you'll weed out ideas that appealed at first but don't wear well over time. I am just so glad I didn't buy that $6,000 hand-carved sandalwood Chinese bed.

GIVE A CUSTOM LOOK TO YOUR HOME
BY ADDING WOODWORK DETAILS
SUCH AS CROWN MOLDING,
WAINSCOTING, AND CHAIR RAILS.

Make the things you love part of your decor. There's no point in collecting vintage linens or antique toys if you never get to see them. Show off your collections and find creative ways to display them.

Replace standard issue hardware or hardware that's at odds with your decor with something that's a better fit. Upgrading cupboard handles, drawer pulls, and doorknobs gives an expensive custom look and underscores your home's unique style.

If you have a fireplace, make it the focal point of the room. Even if it's not a working fireplace, no matter—think of it as a picture frame for you to fill with something beautiful and eye-catching, like a luxurious floral arrangement or an antique quilt displayed to show off its rich colors.

Fill the bare spots on the wall that are crying out for a major piece of art. If you haven't found the right one yet, take the pressure off yourself and try a grouping of smaller, thematically related pictures. If you find the right piece of major art, these fill-ins can be put to use elsewhere. And if you don't find the major piece you're looking for, you might decide you like the arrangement you have, and the impact can be just as dramatic.

When the seasons change, dress your rooms for the season. Lighter curtains and brighter pillows, slipcovers, and throws welcome in spring as winter's on its way out, while switching to accent colors like garnet or topaz set the stage for fall and winter. No matter what the season is, there should be items you look forward to setting out and seeing again.

Grow a few attractive plants in pots and you'll lever be at a loss for indoor flowers. Just arrange them in a wicker basket deep enough to conceal the pots, tuck in some added greenery, and you'll have an impressive display at a moment's notice.

Replace ho-hum overhead lighting in your dining room with a unique chandelier. People often make the mistake of economizing on light fixtures, but you really shouldn't. A good light fixture, especially when other options are limited, should be looked upon as a piece of furniture. No matter what your room's style is, there's a lighting option that will make your heart sing. This strategy has another plus as well—by drawing the eye upward, to the airier parts of the room, the right fixture can make the space feel lighter and larger.

Give your bedroom a luxurious feel by adding an extra set of pillows to the bed and buying the next size larger duvet. You'll never need to fight over the covers again.

Remember all the senses when you create your home. Vary the textures in fabrics and materials, give the nose a bit of a treat by adding vases of fresh flowers and use lamps as well as overhead lighting.

TEMPT THE SENSES

Decorating your home with scent is as important as decorating with color and fabric. Here are a few ways to make your home smell as good as it looks:

→ **Let the sweet smells of summer in** by using fans and cross ventilation and avoiding air conditioning whenever possible.

→ **Find high-quality scented candles** and burn them with abandon. (Tip: Keep your candles in the freezer and they'll burn longer.)

→ **Make your own simmering potpourri** by filling a pot with water and adding citrus rinds, wedges of citrus, or a mix of apple peels and cinnamon sticks. Turn the burner on low and your house will smell delicious—just don't leave it unattended or let it boil dry.

→ **Soak cotton balls in concentrated extracts** such as vanilla, lemon, or orange and tuck them away in a corner. If you have children or pets, guard against accidental ingestion by putting the fragrant balls in any small plastic bottle with a childproof cap, punching numerous holes in the bottle, and making sure the cap is on securely.

My personal favorite is an all-purpose fragrance I use as an after-shower splash and room spritz. To make it, find an old, empty perfume bottle with an atomizer (though any spray bottle will do) and fill it with about a cup of witch hazel (available at any drugstore). Now add a teaspoon or two of pure almond extract. This is especially good for freshening draperies and upholstery, since it's light and fresh and doesn't harm or stain fabric.

{ **Open the windows and air out rooms year round, even during winter.** }

A chair sits beside a small dresser in the corner of this rustic bedroom; the perfect place for the morning ritual of lacing up ones shoes.

HOW TO STAGE A ROOM

Is your furniture pushed back against the walls like bales of hay, waiting for the barn dance to begin? This popular arrangement is also the most misguided. Most people opt for it because they want the room to look spacious, but it never quite delivers on the promise. No matter where you sit, you feel isolated and on the fringes. To make conversation, you have to call across the room. Even if you're in the room alone with a book, the arrangement still doesn't work. There's no sense of coziness—you just feel like the fly on the wall.

And having been a guest in many such rooms, I can tell you that when it comes to mingling, you might as well fill the room with roadblocks. The simple act of going to the buffet table makes you feel as conspicuous as a high school graduate crossing the stage to get a diploma, while the idea of introducing yourself to a stranger on the other side of the room makes you fear being mistaken for a stalker. No wonder people usually end up in the kitchen.

The bare space in the middle of the room becomes an alley people want to pass through as quickly as possible, because there's nothing to keep them there, no objects of interest or comfortable places to perch. To make the room work, you want to reverse the equation, and go back to what Vikings, Native Americans, African villages, and hundreds of other civilizations knew: life takes place in the center of the hut. What you want is to keep the foot traffic on the edges of the room, and cluster people closer to the center. True, you probably don't have a fire pit or cooking fire there to draw the crowd, but you do have furniture. So pull the seating away from the walls and make cluster points where people can gather and talk. A good arrangement is the capital H, with small sofas serving as the two parallel lines and a coffee table creating the connecting bar.

continued on next page

continued from previous page

Chairs flanking a fireplace, positioned to face each other rather than the room, or chairs buttoned together by a small end table—all these simple arrangements work to make a room seem friendly rather than forbidding. Ironically, they work to create something else, too—spaciousness. Pulling the furniture away from the wall creates an extra layer of space that makes the room expand.

Take the time to make a floor plan, drawn to scale, of the rooms you live in. Since this is a bit of work, have several copies made or scan it into your computer and put the original away for safekeeping. Working from your floor plan, draw simple shapes to represent your furniture, and shapes to represent furniture you're thinking of buying. Now you have an easy way to experiment with different arrangements and see how new pieces would fit. It may seem like child's play, but it really does help you get a feel for what will work and what won't.

Match the scale of the furniture to the size of the room. As a rule, a large room will make small-scale pieces look fragile and even cheap, rather than delicate or streamlined. At the other end of the spectrum, large pieces shrink a small room and make it feel cramped.

One way you can make a large piece of furniture work in a small area is to reduce the amount of furniture. If there just a few pieces, the space doesn't feel claustrophobic. If you can resist the urge to add more, your large piece turns into a focal point that makes the room around it seem larger rather than smaller.

Can't afford that major add-on just yet? You may already have the space that will make your home feel larger. It's truly ironic how many people find porches in vintage homes irresistible, but ignore their own porches, decks, and patios. In the past, people revered their porches, and treated them as an extension of the house itself. If you had grandparents with a porch, you probably know what I mean. I remember porches with fancy gliders and round oak tables where summer suppers were eaten. My grandparents' porch had a built-in bench spanning one end, piled high with cushions and pillows, just begging you to stretch out for a nap. Times have changed, but this is one tradition worth bringing back. Chances are your porch, deck, or patio has plenty of space to tap. The trouble is, the space is occupied by a barbecue grill with a weather-rumbled cover, the garden hose that really doesn't belong there, and lawnchairs that have seen better days. Start giving your outdoor space the same care and attention you give your indoor space. Paint or refinish the surface, upgrade the furniture, add some conversation pieces and accessories and "indoor" touches like rugs, tablecloths, and lighting. The area will seem like an extension and your home will feel more spacious, even when you're inside.

{ Big couches flank a chest in the engaging "H" layout. }

WHAT MAKES
A GREAT
GUEST ROOM?

One of the joys of having a clean, well-run, and thoughtfully decorated dwelling is sharing it with guests. You want your friends and relatives to enjoy your home as much as you do, and you want to make their stay special. Having been a guest as well as a host, here's my list of guest room ingredients for a pleasant and memorable stay.

Make the space clean and inviting. It's especially important that a guest room is bright and cheerful. No one likes to feel they've been warehoused in a gloomy, forgotten corner. If your guestroom does happen to be somewhat somber, do a little creative staging, such as tossing a bright throw across the bed, adding an extra lamp, or choosing sheets with a punch of color.

Take away the clutter. Many guest rooms are dual-purpose rooms, and function most of the time as the home office, the sewing room, or the exercise room. Take time to clear out or put away as much of the room's other life before your guests come. Uncluttered also means private— for the length of the stay, family members should find another place to check their email, exercise, and all the rest.

Show your guests they're special. There's a particular kind of happiness that happens when you see something that was put in the room especially for you. It could be a small vase of flowers from the garden, a little coffeemaker with an assortment of coffees, or a few homemade cookies on a pretty plate. Whatever it is, you feel special and welcomed—and how often does that happen in life?

Provide a desk and a chair. Most of us organize ourselves around desks. It's the way we live in the modern world, and not having a familiar place to leave your keys or purse, or sit at while you plan your day, can be a bit disorienting.

Be a good concierge. If your guests are going to go adventuring on their own, give them maps of

A WARM AND INVITING GUEST ROOM
CAN SERVE AS A MULTIPURPOSE
SPACE—ESPECIALLY WHEN DECORATED
WITH A DESK AND CHAIR.

{ **Providing bedtime reading for guests is a must.** }

the area, keys, advice about where to go and what to see—whatever they need to feel enthusiastic about exploring your neck of the woods.

Don't forget the basics. Some people can't fall asleep without the radio, others need to read a bit, and still others have to know what time it is the minute they open their eyes. We all have our little habits and ways of comforting ourselves.

Offer something to read or look at before bed. One of the things I looked forward to most about visiting my favorite aunt was the bedside reading. It was always a book chosen with great care, one she was convinced I should not live without reading, and it always delighted me. I've carried on the tradition of leaving a book or two on the night table,

but I also leave vintage magazines (preferably from the year of my guest's birth), family photo albums when relatives are visiting, and old letters and greeting cards my guest and I exchanged years ago.

Add a "just for you" touch. Everybody likes goodie bags, and putting together a little basket of whimsical treats lets my guests know how happy I am that they've come to see me. Anything can go into the basket, as long as it's inexpensive and not at all practical—little bars of chocolate, crocheted pillowcase edgings for the cousin who has a country-themed home, a ceramic olive tray I got at a flea market for fifty cents, a dummied-up newspaper headline announcing my guests' arrival. It's fun, it feels good, and it gets the visit off to a good start.

BEHIND
THE SCENES

The Elements
of Clean

········ — — — — — — ········

When you think about it, cleaning is really a form of decorating. All of us have been in ordinary and even humble homes that held considerable charm simply because they were faultlessly clean, just as we've seen the charm of otherwise lovely homes ruined by dingy shower curtains, streaky windows, and scuffed floors. So dislike cleaning though you might, the only way to make sure your home's beauty shines through is to master the basic task of keeping it clean.

PREVENTATIVE CLEANING

The best, most efficient way to have a clean home is to keep dirt and mess to a minimum in the first place. With a little thinking ahead, you can cut your cleaning time in half. Here are some of the best ways I know to clean less—and enjoy your home more.

Most household dirt—about 75 to 80 percent—is tracked in from outside. You can keep much of it outdoors where it belongs by cleaning driveways, porches, sidewalks, and garage floors regularly. Oil spills in the garage should be immediately attended to, as oil spreads easily and, once spread, is extremely difficult to remove.

Vacuum or shake entryway rugs and mats at least as often as you vacuum the rest of the house, and wash them once a month (or more, when the weather's been bad). Outdoor mats should also be washed just as frequently. There's no point in leaving the deposited dirt there only to pick it up and track it through the house later.

Visiting relatives in Sweden, I noticed that everyone automatically shed their shoes at the door. No wonder their gleaming wooden floors bore no scuff marks or grit. I brought this tradition home with me.

Position your umbrella stand as close to the door as possible, so you won't have to carry a dripping umbrella into the house. If there's room, keep a few rolled up newspapers concealed in it on which to set wet shoes and boots.

If you have pets that go outdoors, wipe their paws and coats when they come in from a run in nasty weather or a muddy run. The extra few minutes it takes will save a lot of cleaning down the line, and most pets enjoy a nice rubdown with a dry towel.

Pressing that little button to turn on the exhaust fan while you're cooking is one of the most

> Make sure every door has a doormat. If possible, use the double door mat system—one outside the door and a second mat or rug inside. Most people will automatically wipe their feet a second time.

effective steps you can take to a clean home. Smoke and grease are sticky magnets for dirt and dust. Dispersed into the air, some drift into other rooms and settle on furniture.

Have your carpets and area rugs professionally cleaned once or twice a year will reduce your dusting and vacuuming duties throughout the house.

Hardwood rockers on hardwood floors are usually a high-maintenance proposition. Even if the woods are evenly matched, they wear the finish off each other. Save yourself the trouble of re-staining and frequent

IF YOU HAVE A FIREPLACE, YOU CAN KEEP SOOT FROM GATHERING BY THROWING A HANDFUL OF SALT ON THE FIRE.

BE REALISTIC ABOUT THE TIME CLEANING TAKES AND DON'T FRUSTRATE YOURSELF BY TRYING TO CRAM IN TOO MANY TASKS AT ONCE. WHEN TIME IS SHORT, DO WHAT NEEDS DOING MOST.

waxing by covering the bottom of each rocker with a strip of masking tape or painter's tape. Besides keeping both floor and rockers in good shape, the tape repels dust. All you'll need to do is replace it every so often.

HOW TO CLEAN

Sad to say, I reached adulthood without the vaguest notion of how to clean. Much of what I know today I learned from a friend who grew up in a family of eight. Here are some of the best tips he gave me, along with a few I've developed on my own.

Understand the three levels of clean. Level One: Tasks that must be done every day or several times a week; Level Two: Tasks that must be done weekly or monthly; and Level Three: Tasks that must be done once or twice a year.

Make a list of the tasks your home needs to stay in the clean zone and assign each one to a category. Make a plan for how each one will get done. Baking chocolate chip cookies can be left to chance. Cleaning needs to be scheduled.

Have a plan. Don't just say you're going to "do the bedroom" or "clean the bathroom"—make

Gather all the supplies you'll need for the task at hand and keep them together in a caddy or clean bucket so you won't waste time running back and forth for them or wondering where you mislaid the spray cleaner.

WHEN BUYING BOOKCASES
AND STORAGE UNITS, CONSIDER
GLASS-FRONTED DESIGNS.
YOU'LL STILL BE ABLE TO SEE YOUR
BOOKS, AND PUT YOUR FAVORITE
OBJECTS ON DISPLAY, BUT OH,
THE TIME YOU'LL SAVE DUSTING.

a mental list of things you want to accomplish. Is today the day to change the sheets? Dust under the bed? Clear out the medicine cabinet and wash the throw rugs?

Do it all, no matter whatever you decide to clean, even if it's only the cluttered desk. Cleaning one thing halfway, and another thing halfway, means nothing gets completely cleaned, and you never get the satisfaction of seeing the job done right.

Try to vacuum when the natural light in the room is at or near its best. You'll do a better job and won't have to come back for touch-ups.

Remember that the purpose of cleaning is to remove soil and clutter, not shift it around.

Put on the radio or some music while you clean. Music will boost your energy and make you more productive. Avoid the television, though—you'll be tempted to watch it, and even a short glance from time to time slows down your progress.

Don't get sidetracked. Now is not the time to sit down and go through those old magazines or try out a new furniture arrangement. Keep moving and get the cleaning done, then reward yourself with the fun stuff.

Television commercials are so long these days you'd be surprised how much you can get done during them. Before the show starts, plot your course of action—dusting, vacuuming, emptying the dishwasher, or dozens of other small tasks. The minute the commercial starts, get out of your chair and get busy. For every hour of television, you'll gain twenty minutes of cleaning time. A lot of the chores on your to-do list will vanish painlessly, and you will have gotten some exercise in the bargain. If you're watching a TV program with no commercials, find some work you can do while you watch—pay bills, sew on that missing button, or go through those magazines you've been meaning to sort.

Look for opportunities to multitask. Wiping down the tiles, faucets, and soap dish while you're take a shower is a painless way to eliminate a more challenging job later. If you brush your teeth for two minutes twice a day, you've got an extra twenty-four hours a year that could be used wiping down the sink or counters with your free hand.

Dust whenever you see dust. I seldom notice dust when I'm actually dusting. Instead, I notice it when I take something off a shelf, change the bulb in a lamp, or turn on the television. Now I have clean dust wipes stashed discreetly all over the house, ready to go. Whenever I notice the dust, I take an extra minute to wipe it away.

THE ORDER OF CLEAN

When you're going to tackle an entire room, here's the order that's most efficient:

1 Remove anything that doesn't belong in the room.

2 Put away objects that belong in the room but are out of place. Hang up clothes, return books to shelves, put away toys and crafts projects.

3 Gather up rugs, slipcovers, throws, tablecloths, and anything else in the room that needs washing. If you don't have a second set of linens for the room, get the load of laundry going.

4 Start at the top. Dust overhead lighting fixtures, ceiling fans, coffers and open beams, drapery rods and cornices.

5 Unless they are too heavy to handle, take art work, mirrors, pictures, and other ornaments off the walls. Put them in the center of the room (or anywhere away from the walls) and drape a sheet over them.

6 Dust the window frames, door frames, and doors.

7 Dust the walls from top to bottom.

8 By this time, your load of washing should be done. Transfer it to the dryer.

Walls need dusting, too. Not just the far corners, where cobwebs gather, but the entire wall. The easiest way to do this is with a Swiffer-style dry mop. Fit the mop with a fresh dust cloth, swipe the entire wall, working from top to bottom, and discard the cloth when you're finished.

Every home has impossible-to-dust items. Instead of avoiding them, try compressed air. Designed for computer equipment, it's convenient to use and can be found in any office supplies store. It's my favorite way to clean dried flowers, candles, lampshades, intricate vases, figurines, and carved wood pieces.

9 Return mirrors and pictures to the wall, dusting each one as you do.

10 Dust the furniture, lamps, countertops, and electronics in the room. As you go, straighten any areas that need tidying— bookshelves, end tables, knick-knack shelves, and so on.

11 Pick one thing to do in the room that isn't absolutely necessary, such as straightening the drawers, washing the windows, or sorting through a stack of old magazines.

12 Dust the baseboards if they need it.

13 Vacuum upholstered furniture.

14 Vacuum the floor.

15 Open a window to air out the room. If it's cold out, close the door when you leave the room to keep the rest of the house warm.

16 Finish the room's laundry, and return anything that's dry to the room.

17 Close the window and leave the door open.

Use slipcovers to keep your
dining room set pristine.
Just toss them into the laundry
when they get scruffy.

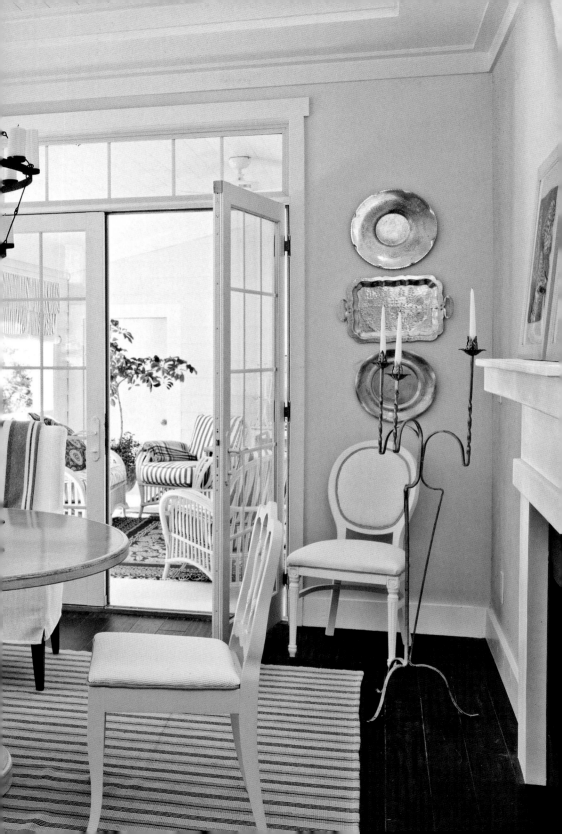

COMPANY COMING AND YOU DON'T HAVE TIME TO SCRUB THE FLOOR? RUN A DAMP MOP AROUND THE EDGES OF THE ROOM, PAYING SPECIAL ATTENTION TO THE CORNERS. PEOPLE WILL THINK THE ENTIRE FLOOR IS SPOTLESS.

There are substance abuse issues concerning compressed air, especially among children and teens, and fatalities have been reported. If you have children in your house, and this is a concern, skip the compressed air and dust the old fashioned way.

Use a padded lint brush to dust fabric lampshades. It's gentle and it works. A conventional dustcloth doesn't work—it either releases the dust into the air or grinds it into the shade—and the upholstery attachment on the vacuum cleaner doesn't suit most shades. So stick with the lint remover.

Book jackets are easy to dust, but the grooves along the top of the pages are a different story altogether. Dust seems to settle there and even a dust-attracting cloth doesn't get it all. The solution is to forget the dustcloth and use a clean, dry paint brush, the same type you'd use with housepaint. The individual bristles dig out the dust, and you can brush vigorously without fear of harming the pages.

Get rid of the smell. Old books, with their stamped leather covers and deckled edges, add interest to any bookshelf. But if that fascinating old volume has a slightly musty smell, you'll want to get rid of the odor. An easy way is to put the books in a brown paper bag with an open box of baking soda, fold the bag closed, and put it away and out of sight for a week or two.

Scratches on a glass-topped table can often be smoothed away with toothpaste. Use traditional paste rather than gel and rub gently. If the scratches aren't too deep, they should be much less noticeable.

Vacuum your couch and upholstered chairs regularly, even if they don't look like they need it. When invisible dirt and dust are left on the surface of the fabric, people sit on it and grind the particles deep into the weave of the fabric. Over time, this builds up and becomes noticeable, and by the time it does, it's too late to vacuum, and even upholstery cleaner might not work.

SIMPLE COUNTRY WISDOM

Do one last thing at night, no matter how tired you are. Whether it's emptying the dishwasher or just wiping the bathroom sink and faucets, it will be one less thing to do tomorrow.

BATHROOM TROUBLE SPOTS

Keeping a bathroom acceptably clean is easy. Taking it to the level of like-new clean is another matter altogether. Below is rapid relief for common ailments such as water spots, mineral deposits, and soap scum.

For natural and continuous air-freshening, douse cotton balls with your favorite fragrant oil and stick one or two in corners and in the medicine cabinet.

Clean the bathroom after your shower or bath, when the steam has loosened the dirt.

Mildew in the grouting between tiles looks like dirt, ranging from gray to black. Eliminating it may not be as difficult as you think. Try the easiest way first—fill a spray bottle with white vinegar and apply directly to the affected grout, wait ten minutes, the rinse. If this doesn't do the trick, dip a clean toothbrush directly into the vinegar and scrub gently. The grout should come clean with surprisingly little effort.

Wash the shower curtains. There are all sorts of home remedies for scrubbing mildew and soap scum from these, most involving a lot of elbow grease. I've had the best results by putting the curtain in the washing machine with ordinary laundry soap and the recommended amount of bleach per load. The bleach eliminates the mildew, while the laundry soap goes after the soap scum, shampoo stains, and all the rest. This method will work on cloth as well as heavier vinyl and plastic.

Prevent mildew in the bathroom with good ventilation. Run the bathroom fan to dry the tub and shower completely after use, and draw the shower curtain closed to prevent mildew from getting a toehold in moist, damp folds. Washing the tub and tiles with a disinfectant cleanser, then rinsing and drying thoroughly, will also help keep mildew at bay.

Rub your ceramic tiles with car wax, let stand for ten minutes, then buff them as you would your car. They'll gleam for you.

To get your cloudy faucets gleaming, you could spend a lot of time scrubbing or you could do what my grandmother did. First, wipe off whatever is easy to

POLISH YOUR BATHROOM MIRROR WITH SHAVING CREAM TO PREVENT IT FROM FOGGING UP. ANY BRAND WILL DO, SO LONG AS IT'S FOAM RATHER THAN GEL, AND THE EFFECT WILL LAST SO LONG AS YOU DON'T RUB THE GLASS.

remove. Next, swab the fixtures liberally with ordinary vinegar. Soak a cloth or paper towel with vinegar and wrap it around the faucet. Go away for an hour— spend some time in the garden, or make those cookies your children have been asking for. After an hour, remove the wrappings and give the fixtures a final rub with a fresh paper towel.

Prevent soap scum and residue from building up on shower doors by getting into the habit of rinsing and wiping them down after each shower.

If soap scum has built up on your shower doors, you've probably already discovered that the usual go-to cleaners aren't especially effective. Odd as it may sound, lemon oil does the trick. If the build up is heavy, it may take a few applications, but soon your doors will be smooth to the touch. Once they're clean, wiping them with the oil once a week should prevent scum from reappearing. Lemon oil will also remove those splotchy water spots on the metal frames around the shower doors.

If mineral deposits have marked the water line of your toilet bowl, add enough water to cover the line, toss in a few denture tablets, let them work overnight, and whisk with the bowl brush in the morning. Repeat if needed, and prevent future stains by repeating weekly.

Mineral deposits that build up inside a showerhead can be easily eliminated. Remove the head and mix one half-cup of vinegar with a quart of very hot water. If the showerhead has plastic parts, soak them in this solution until the water cools. If mineral deposits remain, repeat the treatment. If your shower head is all metal and has no plastic parts to worry about, pour the solution in a saucepan, add the head, and simmer for fifteen to twenty minutes.

Clean the tracks on sliding medicine cabinets and shower doors by wrapping the head of a small brush (such as an old toothbrush) with a reusable wipe that's been moistened with cleaning solution and run it along the troughs of the track.

A FRESHLY LAUNDERED SHOWER CURTAIN WILL BE MORE RESISTANT TO MILDEW IF, IMMEDIATELY AFTER WASHING, IT IS RUBBED WITH LEMON JUICE AND DRIED OUTSIDE, IN FULL SUNLIGHT.

Bothered by those impossible-to-clean spots in tight corners? Spray with cleaner, give it a minute to loosen the dirt, then clean with a cotton swab.

If you have a tiled floor, dirt and talcum powder can work their way into the crevices, especially where the floor joins the tub or meets the baseboard. To avoid scrubbing on your hands and knees, do this first: broom the crevices and trouble spots with a clean, dry paint brush. An inexpensive model three or four inches wide will do the trick. Then sweep or vacuum as usual and washing the floor will be a snap.

THE WAY WITH WINDOWS

Nothing is as pleasing as clean, sparkling windows. Yet with all our modern products, this simple goal isn't always easy to achieve. When clear as glass isn't clear at all, it's time to go back to the basics. Here's what you need to know.

If your windows always seem dirty, the reason may have nothing to do with your cleaning methods. When was the last time you checked the filters in the heating and air conditioning systems? Most of us don't clean and replace these as often as we should, and this means more dirt, dust, and pollen stays in our indoor air and, eventually, migrates to the windows. While you're at it, check to make sure registers and vents are clean as well, so you aren't inadvertently blowing dust back into the air.

Pick your cleaning day. There's a natural instinct to wash windows on a brilliantly sunny day. Unfortunately, this is the worst weather for the job. Bright sunlight causes the glass to dry quickly, which promotes streaking. Choose a cloudy day for your work, or do it late in the day, when direct sunlight no longer strikes the glass.

Remember the squeegee. Invented over seventy years ago, the squeegee is still the weapon

THE ELEMENTS OF CLEAN

of choice among those who clean windows for a living. If the only examples you've seen of this single-bladed piece of rubber fitted with a handle are industrial-sized, take another look. Squeegees come in all widths, including sizes small enough to fit into tiny-paned windows. They're also available with extenders, so you can reach tall windows without a ladder. In addition to their cleaning powers, squeegees are friendly to the environment and the family budget, since you won't need paper towels or window spray. Here's a tip from the pros: clean and dry a one-inch strip at the top of each window first; starting a squeegee on a thoroughly dry surface will prevent drips.

Homemade is still the best.
Since windows collect not only dust but the film of cooking and nicotine, if there's a smoker in the house, cleaning solution needs to be more than just a polisher. I've found that homemade solutions work best for this. The recipe I use is quick and easy to mix: combine one-third cup of water with one-third cup of rubbing alcohol and add one teaspoon of white vinegar. There are many other good homemade recipes as well, and the ones I've tried all work well. Besides getting the glass clean, they do not streak, as commercial products frequently do. There is, however, one drawback. Almost all homemade solutions contain ingredients such as vinegar, alcohol, or ammonia that will harm your woodwork, so you will need to carefully apply small amounts by hand or mask your woodwork with painter's tape. On the upside, homemade remedies seem to keep glass cleaner longer, so you'll be able to get by with fewer cleanings.

For perfect, clear windows,
and for everyone who's ever gone back and forth trying to figure out which side the stubborn streak is on, try this: use vertical strokes on one side of the glass and horizontal strokes on the other. The direction of the streak will tell you which side needs attention.

If smudge marks develop between washings, try spot
cleaning. Finger and paw prints may come off simply by swiping with an old-fashioned chalkboard eraser—just make sure it's never been used, or you'll be spreading chalk dust. If the mark isn't erasable, dab with a little isopropyl alcohol and rub dry.

NOTHING POLISHES GLASS LIKE GOOD OLD-FASHIONED NEWSPAPER. JUST BE SURE NOT TO USE ANY SHEETS WITH COLORED PICTURES ON THEM.

There are two reasons why frost forms on the inside of windows in cold weather. The first is that your humidifier is set too high, and needs to be lowered as the outside temperature drops. The second is inadequate insulation. While you can't eliminate this problem without addressing the underlying cause, using isopropyl alcohol to polish the inside of the pane will help.

Windows are part of your home's overall climate system. Strategically positioned window fans can draw air through the house on days that might otherwise require air conditioning—and who wouldn't rather live with fresh air and the nostalgic hum of a fan than the antiseptic chill of that giant appliance?

CURTAINS AND TRIM

Those little discolorations that appear on aluminum window frames are oxidation. To keep them from forming, wash and dry the frames thoroughly, then apply car wax to the frames. Do this once a year and you will never see a freckled frame again.

If oxidation discolorations have already appeared on your aluminum frames, first try washing them away with liquid detergent. If this doesn't work, try wetting the spot, then applying a mildly abrasive cleanser and rubbing with a cloth. Don't use steel wool or abrasive cleansers that might scratch.

The fastest and most effective way to dust blinds is to put on a pair of inexpensive soft cotton gloves, give them a shot of dusting spray, and glide your fingers over the slats. I actually have a few pairs of gloves, so if they get too soiled, I can switch to a clean pair. When I'm finished, I just toss them in the laundry.

Can't get your curtain tie-backs evenly positioned? Forget about yardsticks and pencil marks on your woodwork. Lower the shade or blinds to the level you want the ties and use it as a guide on both sides—your tie-backs will be perfect.

Get into the habit of adjusting shades and blinds to moderate your home's energy. Blinds are especially effective because, in addition to being raised and lowered, the slats can be adjusted to deflect harsh sun while still letting light into the room. In cold winter months, lowering shades and blinds as soon as the sun sets provides an extra barrier of protection against the seeping cold.

Let some fresh air in if the weather outside cooperates.
There's nothing like that first breeze in autumn.

WHEN WOODEN WINDOWSILLS AND WINDOW SHUTTERS GET DIRTY AND DUSTY TOO QUICKLY, GIVE THEM A COAT OF FLOOR WAX BOTH INSIDE AND OUT.

Curtains help control indoor climate. Bright, light-colored fabrics reflect sunlight and encourage air flow. In cold climates, heavy drapes absorb the cold air that lingers around windows. You may want to consider having two sets of window treatments, and changing them with the seasons. If this isn't practical, simply making curtain liners of heavy fabric and threading them on an expansion rod, which can easily be popped in and out of the window, will go a long way to saving energy in the winter.

The Tao of Laundry

E.B. White, author of *Charlotte's Web*, had a marvelous approach to life: "We should all do what, in the long run, gives us joy, even if it is only picking grapes or sorting the laundry." I confess that the laundry does give me joy. It seems to me one of the more painless household chores, maybe because I harbor distant memories of my grandmother making her own lye soap and my mother trying, often without success, to free some article of clothing from the maws of a wringer washing machine. Laundry has come a long way, and the return—clean clothes, fragrant sheets and towels—seems like a great bargain for a modest investment of time. If you don't quite love laundry day, here are some tips that will lighten your work load.

THE WAY WE WASH

When you take off a pair of socks, pin them together with a safety pin before you throw them in the hamper. It will save you two sortings—once when you do the washing and another when you're folding and putting away dry laundry.

My mother was a great believer in soaking, long before pre-treatment sprays. Simply filling a tub with water and letting

clothes bathe overnight goes a long way toward loosening dirt and grime, giving your washing machine a head start on doing its job. It's especially effective when your clothes aren't stained but have that dingy-all-over look.

Why do shirt and blouse collars get so grimy? Body oils rub onto the collar and attract dirt. To get the collar clean, you have to dissolve the oils. The solution isn't in your laundry room, but your bathroom. Grab your shampoo and a clean paintbrush and paint a line of shampoo over the soiled collar before washing.

Liquid dish soap works as well, and sometimes better, than many of the pretreatment sprays for most food stains. First, blot the spot with cool water to remove as much of the stain as possible. Then dab the spot with a small amount of liquid dish soap and let sit for about half an hour. Don't rub, just let the soap do its work, then rinse in cool water and blot again. If the stain still doesn't come out, repeat the process but give the soap several hours or overnight to work.

Didn't get to soak a bloodstain in cold water before the blood dried? Before putting it in the wash, dampen with hydrogen peroxide, then rinse with cold water. If possible, set the wash temperature for cold as well. Even if it doesn't lift the stain completely, it will lighten it considerably. Repeat the peroxide treatments with each wash.

If you've washed a stained garment, examine the results before tossing it in the dryer. If the stain didn't come out, the dryer's heat will set it and make it even harder to deal with. Your chances of success are greater if you re-treat the item while it's still damp.

We've all sent something through the dryer only to discover a stain later on. When that happens, your best chance of rescue is to soak for thirty minutes in a solution that is half water, half hydrogen peroxide, then wash immediately. Hydrogen peroxide is strong, so this isn't recommended for fragile fabrics.

If you use bleach on your whites, they will eventually acquire a dingy, discolored look. To remedy the problem, let the washing machine fill with water, add one-half to one cup of hydrogen peroxide to the load (depending on the volume of water, not the dinginess of the items) and

soak for half an hour. After thirty minutes, add about one-third less laundry detergent than usual and wash as usual.

Laundry can develop a stale, musty smell, especially in the summer months. Adding a quarter cup of ordinary baking soda to the wash will freshen both the clothes and the machine itself.

How you load your machine matters. Take the time to straighten sleeves and pant legs, close zippers and fastenings, and untangle sheets and towels. Clothes will get cleaner, keep their shape better, develop fewer wrinkles, and get drier during the spin cycle.

Separate clothes by fabric type as well as by color. Don't wash heavyweight fabrics with delicate sheers, and separate towels and fleeces from smooth dark fabrics that show every speck of lint.

For stubborn food stains, such as coffee, soy sauce, or mustard, try foam shaving cream.

A CUP OF VINEGAR, ADDED DURING THE RINSE CYCLE, IS A PERFECT NATURAL FABRIC SOFTENER. IT'S ESPECIALLY GOOD TO SOFTEN AND PLUMP UP TOWELS, WHICH COMMERCIAL SOFTENERS CAN SOMETIMES MAKE A BIT TOO TAME.

TO DISCOURAGE LINT, ADD A CUP OF WHITE VINEGAR TO THE WASH.

Follow the instructions for liquid dish soap on page 96, giving the foam at least an hour to work.

To keep black clothes from fading, turn them inside out and choose the coolest temperature setting that will get them clean.

If you're washing heavy items that take a long time to dry, running them through an extra spin cycle before taking them out of the washer will reduce drying time.

If a garment bleeds onto other items in the load, don't let the stained items dry. Instead, was them again immediately with detergent and a color-safe bleach—and without the garment that caused the trouble.

After you empty your washing machine, check the inside and wipe up any lint, threads, or traces of detergent that are left behind. Also wipe around the rim of the bucket, where soil can build up. Wiping with a cloth or paper towel moistened with vinegar will keep mildew from gaining a toehold. When you're finished, leave the door or lid open so the interior can dry thoroughly.

Clean your washing machine of soap residue every so often by running an empty cycle of hot water to which a quart of vinegar has been added.

If you've dyed clothing in your machine and the dye has left stains, run an empty cycle of hot water with two cups of bleach added. If traces of the dye remain, repeat the process but let the

How many times have you found a button in the bottom of your washer, dryer, or laundry basket and had no idea where it came from? Keep a small plastic container or zip-style plastic bag nearby to keep the strays in, and when you find the garment that's missing its button, you'll know where to look.

diluted bleach soak in the machine for several hours.

I enjoy doing hand laundry, especially on a hot day when the touch of cool water is delightful and refreshing. But I always seem to add too much detergent, leaving me with suds that are hard to rinse out. A friend told me to try adding a little vinegar to the rinse water. The verdict: it works.

Sweaters and knits absorb an incredible amount of water. No matter how much water you squeeze out, the garment is still so saturated and heavy that hanging it up would pull it out of shape. I finally solved this problem by buying a mesh shopping bag. Now I place the garment in the bag, hang the bag in the shower, and let it drip until it's dry enough to lay out or hang.

Save energy by letting laundry partially dry on a rack before finishing in a dryer. According to energy experts, you can cut dryer costs 25 to 75 percent this way.

IN THE DRYER

Take a moment with each garment and you'll save on wrinkles. Straighten out wadded-up sleeves and pant legs and untwist garments that have gotten bunched up. Give the garment a few snaps before adding it to the dryer, and you'll find folding and ironing a much easier task.

Dry like with like. Synthetics and very lightweight natural fabrics can be dried together on the permanent press cycle, while sheer and fragile fabrics may do with a short tumble in cool air. Even cotton fabrics should be sorted by weight to avoid overdrying lightweight items and needlessly prolonging the drying time of heavier fabrics.

Get the load right. You'd think drying just a few items in a load would speed the drying time, wouldn't you? Well, odd as it seems, the answer is no. Too few clothes reduces the tumbling action, which lengthens drying time. On the other hand, an overloaded dryer is also inefficient—air doesn't circulate evenly and clothes may emerge with damp patches. Even if clothes are dry, they may be more wrinkled than need be. Find out what the optimum capacity is for your dryer and load it accordingly.

Drying two loads back to back is more efficient than drying them at different times because the dryer only needs to heat up once. If you do a double batch, do the lighter-weight clothes first. The dryer will be thoroughly

CLOTHES THAT ARE PRONE TO FADING WILL FADE LESS IF YOU TURN THEM INSIDE OUT BEFORE LOADING THEM IN THE DRYER.

BEFORE STARTING THE DRYER, CHECK TO MAKE SURE THE VENT ISN'T BLOCKED AND THE LINT BASKET IS CLEAN. OVERLOOKING THESE BASICS LENGTHENS DRYING TIME, COSTS MONEY, AND WASTES ENERGY.

heated, and it will shorten the drying time of the heavier items.

When drying heavy items such as blue jeans, rugs, or blankets, add a clean, dry bath towel to the load. The fluffier the towel, the better—it will absorb extra moisture and reduce drying time.

Reduce static cling by removing items from the dryer before they are bone dry.

There are all sorts of methods for drying down items, from adding a tennis ball to adding a sneaker. But really, neither of these items was intended for the dryer, and both can spread dye and dirt, and even begin to melt. It's a better idea to throw a few clean, dry bath towels in with the down item to absorb moisture, and stop the dryer from time to time to remove the item and shake vigorously to make sure the down isn't clumping.

THE LOST ART OF LINE DRYING

Who should line dry their laundry? Almost everyone. Between the energy dryers take and the damage they do to clothes, line drying is a huge money-saver. Just two caveats: First, if you or anyone you live with has asthma or allergies, line drying usually isn't a good idea because pollen drifting through the air gets caught on clothes and stays there. Also, some communities have banned clotheslines as unsightly, although many have had to lift such bans due to public pressure. So before putting up lines, check to see where your community stands. If you do line dry, here are some tips for smooth sailing.

Make sure your laundry lines are strong and taut. Laundry doesn't dry evenly on sagging lines, and this will cause you more work.

{ Clean your clothespins. Place them in a mesh bag, swish in a bucket of warm sudsy water, rinse thoroughly, then hang the whole bag on the line to dry. }

The key to less ironing is good hanging, so it's worth taking the time to do it right. First, shake each item to release wrinkles. Shake delicate items and knits gently. Give heavier items a good shake that makes them snap. Then smooth and straighten each garment as you hang it. No twisted sleeves, turned back cuffs, rumpled collars, or wadded pocket linings, please!

Make use of every inch of line. If you have the space, leave a foot or two between items. They'll dry faster.

Hang sheets and whites in the sunlight early in the morning to get the full bleaching effect of the sun's rays. Hang colors and brights in partial shade or in the afternoon, after the sun has passed its zenith, to prevent fading.

Prevent colored clothes from fading by turning them inside out before hanging.

Hang your shirts and blouses on hangers with the top button buttoned to prevent clothespin marks on the shoulders. Hook and pin the hangers on the line.

When the weather is raw and chilly, put on a pair of thin, lightweight cotton or knit gloves, then add a pair of rubber gloves over them—you fingers will stay dry and toasty.

Choose a day that's sunny and windy or at least breezy. The motion of the breeze prevents clothes from stiffening. If you do have a good breeze going, leaving items on the line a few hours after they're dry will make them all the softer.

ONCE A MONTH, USE A RAG TO GO OVER YOUR OUTDOOR CLOTHESLINES WITH WARM WATER AND PINE OIL CLEANER. DIRTY CLOTHESLINES WILL GET YOUR CLOTHES DIRTY AS WELL.

TWELVE GOOD REASONS TO LINE DRY

1 Conserving energy saves you money. It isn't just the planet you're helping out, it's your own finances. Use of dryers account for 50 to 65 percent of the average household's electric bill, and that doesn't count the extra air conditioning you may need to counteract the heat the dryer puts out.

2 Clothes last longer. You know the gobs of lint you pull out of the dryer filter? Those are bits of your clothes, fluffed and shredded from continuous rubbing against each other. The unsightly pills that send otherwise good clothes into early retirement have the same cause. Dryer heat is especially hard on spandex and elastic, so line drying means basics like socks, undies, and lingerie won't have to be replaced nearly as often.

3 Say goodbye to shrinking and set-for-life stains. Unless you wash a dry-clean-only item by mistake, shrinkage almost always happens during drying, not washing. And once a garment shrinks, it will never be the same again. The same thing goes for stains. Wash cycles are seldom hot enough to set an untreated stain, but dryer cycles can make it permanent.

4 Sunlight has a gentle, natural bleaching effect. Nothing gets whites whiter or prevents yellowing as effectively.

5 Save on anti-static sheets. Clothes that hang dry don't develop static cling.

6 Line drying cools the yard down. Air passing over wet cloth has a decidedly cooling effect. Compare your backyard on a hot summer day to your backyard on a hot summer day when laundry is drying. The difference is astounding. Depending on where your clothesline is positioned, it can even shade and cool a wall of your house.

7 Line drying also cools you down. On a hot dry day, hanging damp laundry is cooling and refreshing.

8 No need to schedule your day around the laundry. Line-dried items will be fine left on the line a few extra hours. You don't have to be on hand to get them out of the dryer before they wrinkle.

9 Line-dried items, especially sheets, are much easier to fold than the tangled mass that comes out of the dryer.

10 It's good for your body. The bending, stretching, and lifting it takes to get laundry on the line is a good way to get in some exercise, without even realizing it.

11 Usually, you can multi-task while hanging your laundry outside and use the time to accomplish some other vital task—like watching your dog scamper and roll in the grass, teaching your children to play hide-and-seek in valleys of billowing sheets, and getting your own dose of relax-and-refresh aromatherapy as you inhale the scent of fresh laundry and soak up the sun's vitamin D.

12 And finally, the best reason of all—have you ever slept on sheets dried in the sun? Pure heaven.

LINENS THAT NEED IRONING (SUCH AS DISHTOWELS, TABLECLOTHS, AND PILLOWCASES) WILL BE EASIER TO WORK WITH IF YOU ROLL THEM RATHER THAN FOLD THEM WHEN YOU TAKE THEM IN.

The hanger method should also be used for lightweight knits to help them keep their shape. Heavy knits like sweaters should not be line dried.

Sheets will dry smoother if you follow this procedure. First, fold the sheet horizontally, hem to hem. Now, turn about four inches of the folded edge over the line and pin. Run your hands down the selvages to make sure they aren't crumpled, and along the hems as well. Not only will the sheets dry more smoothly, but when it's time to take them in, your folding job is already half done.

Don't hang bath towels by the corners—their relatively heavy weight will pull the corners out of shape and leave permanent indents that spoil their look. Instead, double them over the line.

Before you throw away that stained or dingy item, launder and hang it in the sun for a full day. If you're lucky, the sun may have bleached out the stain and lightened the dinginess.

Is your laundry stiff when you take it off the line? The most likely cause is that you used too much soap in the wash. Heavy items like jeans and bath towels will stiffen a bit even if you used the right amount of soap. To soften them, tumble in the dryer on cool for a few minutes.

IRONING

If you don't have time to iron right away, hang your laundry anyway, preferably while it's still warm. A lot of the wrinkles will smooth out on their own.

If items have developed wrinkles from being left to cool in the dryer or laundry basket, put them back in the dryer and tumble until warm. Hang, iron, or fold immediately.

Fold small items such as towels, pillow cases, and T-shirts on top of the warm dryer. The heat will help smooth away wrinkles and you won't need to iron them at all.

Before you begin to iron, go over your ironing board cover with a damp cloth to remove any lint, dust, or stray pet hair.

Iron items that need the least heat first, moving on to those that need hotter, then the hottest, settings. Since irons require a good deal of electricity to heat, you'll be conserving energy.

All fabrics, and the thread they're woven from, have a finish to them. Some cotton garments feel almost nubby, while others feel smooth to the point of silky. To avoid spoiling the finish, it's important to iron with smooth, even strokes. Keep the iron moving, preferably with the grain of the fabric, and avoid pressing too hard or going back and forth over such a small area that heat builds up in the fabric underneath the iron.

To iron a shirt or blouse, begin with the underside of the collar, then the upper side. Do the sleeves next, back first, then the front. Then do the back of the garment (yoke first, body next), then the front inside facings, and finish with the exterior front.

To iron a dress, do the bodice first, in the order described above, then do the skirt.

When faced with pleats, most people instinctively start at the top and iron down, either holding the pleat in place by hand or trying a whole host of time-consuming shortcuts, ranging from clothespins to paper clips to tape. Invariably, the effort goes awry and the pleat meanders off course. This is one time when

TO PRESS ITEMS MADE FROM DARK FABRICS OR SYNTHETIC BLENDS, IRON INSIDE OUT SO THEY WON'T DEVELOP A SHEEN.

instinct should not prevail. For easier ironing, start at the bottom of the pleat and iron up. Your pleats will be perfectly straight with far less effort.

For perfectly pressed slacks, iron the

inside pockets first, then the waistband, backside, and front down to the crotch. Lay the slacks out with the inside seams together. Straighten and smooth the legs carefully, then peel back the top leg and press the inseam side of the bottom leg. Press from the seam out, smoothing and adjusting as you go to create straight creases front and back. Last, press the side seam portion of each leg. Now comes the most important step—hang them up by the cuffs immediately. Draping them over or chair or folding over a hanger, even for a few minutes, will spoil your hard work.

Items prone to excessive wrinkling should be removed

from the dryer when they're still a bit damp and hung up to finish drying naturally. They'll be far easier to iron.

Instead of using the steam feature on your iron, mix one

part fabric softener with five parts water and use it to spray laundry as you iron. Wrinkles will be easier to get rid of, and your clothes will smell wonderful.

Linens and cottons will be

easier to iron if you moisten them with a spray mist, bundle them in a plastic bag, then chill them in your refrigerator for several hours. We don't know why it works, but it does.

I love using tablecloths, but

ironing them is another matter—it can seem a bit like raising sails in a gale force wind, and I often end up with more wrinkles than when I started. Then someone told me how to do it right. First, make the tablecloth the last item you iron. Fold the cloth in half lengthwise, mist well, and iron from the edge to the center, stopping about six inches short of the fold. Now flip the cloth over and iron the other side. Finally, open the cloth and press straight down the center— the tablecloth is perfectly ironed, without a single crease. Let it cool on the board, then transfer it to the table or fold and put away. If you fold the cloth, it will develop a few gentle fold marks, but they will be much easier to smooth away than wrinkles that formed in the course of ironing.

To *remove a stubborn wrinkle* from lace or any delicate fabric you don't want the iron to touch directly, mist a clean handkerchief with water, lay it over the item, and press gently. The wrinkle should disappear, and your delicate garment won't be harmed.

After ironing, let garments cool completely on hangers before transferring to your closet or wearing. They'll be less prone to wrinkling, and look crisp longer.

If you're packing for a trip, fold your ironed clothes lengthwise rather than crosswise—when you hang them up, the creases will be more likely to disappear.

For me, the great event of the twentieth century was somebody figuring out how to fold a fitted sheet. To do the trick, put one corner of the sheet over your hand, right side out. Now, put either of the adjacent corners over the first corner, inside out, so that the right sides are together. Now do the same with the other two corners, so that you have two sets of corners. Now fit one set of corners over the other, smoothing the turned-down edge of the sheet so it lies flat. Fold into quarters and you have a reasonably tidy, easy-to-stack bundle.

Tuck pillowcases between the folds of the sheet they match, and keep top and bottom sheets together, so you can easily find a complete set when you're changing sheets.

When returning sheets and towels to the linen closet, put the clean items at the bottom of the stack. This way, everything will get used before it gets stale from sitting in the closet too long.

Store linens together by season; then you will not have to dig through your summer sheets to find your heavier winter ones, and your cold weather throws will not be far from your holiday tablecloths. This is especially efficient if you have a deep linen closet. Take an hour when the seasons change to move the waning season's linens to the back, and bring forward the items you'll be using in the coming months. Not only will everything be within easy reach when you need it, but you can pull out linens ahead of time to make sure nothing needs mending or washing.

IN THE KITCHEN

6

Kitchen Wisdom

To me, of all the rooms in the house, the kitchen is the one that must be well-managed. It's the heart of the home, and reflects the overall spirit of the place. The kitchen is where most of the family conversation goes on, where we gather to nourish our bodies and share the events of the day, where we're most likely to sit with friends over a cup of coffee. Some people treasure the first scent of morning coffee as it mingles with the flooding sunlight. I like the kitchen best at night, with everything cleaned and put away, the whole room lit by the dim glow of the stove hood and stars winking outside the window.

ORGANIZATION & MANAGEMENT

Arrange your kitchen to keep equipment, utensils, and ingredients as close to where you'll use them as possible. Keep plastic wrap and plastic containers for leftovers near the fridge, flour and sugar canisters near your mixer and baking counter, and ladles and spatulas near the stove.

Every kitchen needs a junk drawer, but it doesn't have to be junky. Use expandable dividers to organize and separate items. What's the point of having a really good stash of junk if you can't find what you want when you need it?

Keep a running inventory of the contents of your freezer on the side of the fridge. How many times have you thrown out freezer-burned items that got lost—and forgotten about—at the back of the freezer? Cross out items as you use them, and add new items as they go in.

When you buy fresh meat to rewrap and freeze, snip the label off the supermarket wrapper and toss it in the freezer bag with the meat. Then you'll know what the item is, how much there is of it, and when you bought it.

> Buying in bulk saves money and time-consuming trips to the grocery store, but keeping all those large boxes and bottles within easy reach can be a challenge. The answer: store dry goods in smaller plastic containers, and anything liquid in salad dressing-sized bottles, and transfer the cumbersome boxes to harder-to-reach shelves.

Keep a pantry inventory too. When you use the next-to-last can or jar of something from the pantry, add it to your grocery list.

Make the most of shelf space by storing lids to your plastic containers in a plastic bin of their own, and keep the bottoms in nested stacks.

Free up drawer and cupboard space by hanging cookware
and utensils on the walls or from racks.

WHEN YOU TRY A RECIPE AND DON'T LIKE IT, THROW AWAY THE CARD OR MAKE A NOTE IN YOUR COOKBOOK. YOU WON'T LIKE IT ANY BETTER THE NEXT TIME AROUND.

Choose square or rectangular storage containers instead of round ones. They're easier to stack, less likely to tip over, and provide much more storage capacity for the space they take up.

Expandable wire racks can double your cupboard space, while attractive countertop units can actually add to the decor. I have a corner countertop shelf that's perfect for cookbooks, and keeps them safe and dry when I spill something on the counter.

Sponges and dishcloths need to be disinfected daily. There are all sorts of ways to do this—including soaking in diluted bleach solution and zapping in the microwave. Perhaps the easiest way is to simply toss them in the dishwasher and run them through with the last load of the day. To make sure the dish cloth gets completely clean, I use safety pins to hang it from the upper rack, clothesline style.

Countertops are magnets for stray objects that don't really belong there. Once a month, remove everything from your kitchen counters and clean them.

When it's time to put things back, put back only what truly belongs there. Find a home for the remaining items or throw them away.

Keep walls, countertops, and floors clean longer by running the exhaust fan when you cook. It will remove most of those tiny grease particles that settle and become sticky little magnets for dust and grime.

Unpack your groceries and put them away immediately. Don't leave boxes on the counter or sacks of canned goods on the floor to "take care of later." Now is the time.

If your community recycles, have a system. I usually keep a sack for paper in the kitchen broom closet. Cans and bottles get taken out every night, since their bulk fills up space fast.

Flatten empty food boxes and cartons before throwing them away. You'll be able to fit far more in your trash or recycle bin.

Check the fridge and freezer for stale or spoiled food that needs to be tossed when the trash is ready to be taken out.

Keep the kitchen drain clear and fresh by throwing in a handful of baking soda and rinsing with hot water.

Take an extra few minutes at night to clean the sink and faucets. Wash and disinfect the counters, and wipe the fridge and the stove (the front as well as the top). Give the floor a sweep, straighten the rug, and fill the pets' bowl with fresh water. Your work is done.

KEEPING APPLIANCES AND TOOLS CLEAN

A clean garbage disposal begins with a pitcher of homemade lemonade. Make as usual, combine with ice cubes in a glass, and have a nice, cool drink. When you're completely refreshed, throw one or two of the used lemons into the disposal and grind. See how easy it is?

For firmer, fresher fruits and vegetables, line your refrigerator crisper with paper towels. The towels will absorb excess moisture and your fruits and vegetables will keep their snap.

If your refrigerator has become musty or outright smelly, place fresh coffee grounds in a saucer and put it on a lower shelf. The smell should be gone within a week. If it isn't, replace with fresh grounds and check to make sure the source of the odor has been thrown out. Once the smell is taken care of, an open box of baking soda in the fridge will keep it smelling fresh.

When you clean your fridge, don't forget to wash the seals as well. Use a small, clean brush to gently sweep away crumbs and dirt caught in the grooves of the seal.

STOVE

If you have a white enamel stove, a gentle, effective, earth-friendly cleaner is always at your fingertips. Just make a paste of baking soda and water, wipe the range top and doors until clean, and finish by going over with a clean, damp cloth or sponge to remove any residue. Your stove will gleam.

Make cleaning a grease-splattered oven easy on yourself. Before you go to bed, pour about a cup of ammonia in an aluminum cake pan and put it in the oven. (The oven should be off, and cool.) Be sure to close the oven door. In the morning, remove the pan

and discard the ammonia. Your oven will wipe clean with a damp sponge. Do this once every three or four weeks and you may never have to resort to chemical oven cleaners.

Keep drips and splattering to a minimum:
Place a pan with a bit of water on the rack below anything you think might drip or bubble over, such as fruit pies. The drips go into the water, there's no scorching smell, and the cleanup is easy.

If you end up with melted plastic
on your oven racks, there's an easy way to deal with it. First, using a pair of kitchen shears, snip as much of the cooled, hardened plastic away as possible. Put the rack back in the oven and turn the oven on. When the plastic that remains is warm and pliant, use a metal putty knife to scrape it away.

Don't use window spray
on the window of your oven. The spray causes brown spots to form and, as I discovered, you will never get them off. Instead, wipe your oven window with warm water and a little dish soap. If this doesn't do the job, try a little vinegar on a paper towel. If the spots are inside the glass, the whole oven door must be taken apart and the glass carefully removed and cleaned.

Touchpads on stoves,
microwaves, and other appliances can be a cleaning challenge. You don't want to use too wet a cloth because water might damage the electronics. I've found the best method is to avoid water altogether. I put a little vinegar on a soft cloth and wipe the touch pad gently.

The easiest way to clean the microwave
is to place a small dish of vinegar in it and zap on High until the vinegar begins to boil. Generously wet a cloth or sponge in the vinegar and wipe the microwave clean.

If your dishwasher isn't cleaning
your glassware quite as well as it once did, it may be because of a gradual buildup of soap residue. To blast the buildup, run a cup of vinegar through an entire cycle when the dishwasher is empty. If this doesn't do the trick, repeat. Do this every four to six weeks (depending on how much use your dishwasher gets) to keep the problem from recurring.

SOAK THE POTS

When confronted with food burned onto pots and pans, my first option is to try soaking in warm sudsy water. If that doesn't work, I try one of these:

1 **Fill the pan with water** and throw in a denture tablet.

2 **Sprinkle the pot with dishwasher powder,** add water, bring it to a boil, then turn down the heat and let it simmer for a few minutes.

3 **Add a handful of baking soda,** fill halfway with water, and boil for ten minutes or so.

4 **If any of these methods doesn't work** completely the first time, I keep at it. It may take a bit longer, but I still prefer it to harsh chemicals.

To clean the reservoir of a coffee maker, drop a denture tablet into it, pour in hot water, and run the brew cycle. Discard the water and wash the glass pot when finished. This will work for coffeemakers up to ten cups. For larger-capacity coffeemakers, add another denture tablet.

Put one cup of uncooked white rice in your coffee grinder and grind as you would beans. This not only cleans the unit but sharpens the blades.

Use a toothbrush to scrub the small holes of a garlic press. A toothbrush is also great for cleaning strainers, sieves, colanders, and graters.

If particles of dough or food are stuck like glue to the countertop, try this: soak a terry cloth kitchen towel under very hot water. Wring it out so it doesn't drip, then spread it over the counter. Press a cookie sheet down on top and leave it for several minutes. When you come back, the

{ If your wooden cutting board or rolling pin has darkened or become discolored, rub with half a lemon, then rinse with clear water. Do this regularly and eventually the wood will be lighter and brighter. }

hot towel should have loosened the food considerably, and your counter will be easy to clean.

Allow metal baking sheets and cake pans to cool completely before washing them. Washing them while they're still warm will cause the metal to warp, and it will never bake evenly again.

If your aluminum pans have lost their luster, try boiling apple peels in them to restore their sheen. To keep them bright after each washing, wipe them with lemon juice and dry thoroughly.

Brown spots that have become baked onto glass pans and casserole dishes can be removed over time. Each time you wash them, spend some time scouring them with a toothbrush and a paste made of baking soda and water. Over time, you'll get the stains off. To keep those brown spots from forming in the first place, spray your glass bakeware with cooking spray or grease it with a thin gloss of oil before baking in it.

Spots on pots are easier to scrub away if you first fill the pot halfway with a solution of one part white vinegar to eight parts water, then boil the mixture in the pot.

THE JOY OF CAST IRON

You will save a lot of scrubbing and scraping if you cook in well-seasoned cast iron. A pan that's been cared for over the years develops a cooking surface that is almost impervious and requires very little oil to cook with. A well-seasoned skillet or Dutch oven will give you crisp fried chicken with just a few spoonfuls of oil, while a griddle will give you evenly browned pancakes with no oil at all. Cast iron is also extremely versatile, and the one pan to have if space is at a premium. The same skillet that pops perfect popcorn

WHETHER YOUR CAST IRON POTS WERE INHERITED FROM YOUR GRANDMOTHER OR YOU SEASONED THEM YOURSELF, COOKING WITH THIS VERSATILE METAL WILL SIMPLIFY—AND ADD TO—YOUR COOKING EXPERIENCE.

can double as a wok and turn into a baking dish for biscuits and cornbread.

The best way to get a good piece of seasoned cast iron is to inherit one, or to get lucky at a garage or estate sale. On the other hand, it's rewarding to buy a piece fresh from the factory and season it yourself over the years. Whichever route is available, take it. You'll never regret your investment of time and effort. Follow these guidelines and you and your cast iron will live—and cook—happily ever after.

When you buy cast iron advertised as preseasoned, the seasoning process is not complete. The manufacturer's treatment has gotten you off to a good start, but the cookware is still relatively raw. It's steel gray in color, may feel rough to the touch, and food will no doubt stick to it. Don't be disappointed. True seasoning is something only time and use can accomplish. Over the years, your cookware will turn from dark gray to deep black. The cooking surface will become smooth to the touch, and food will not stick to it.

PROTECT YOUR CAST IRON

Once your cast iron is well on the road to becoming a treasured heirloom, keep it that way. Here are a few "don'ts" to be aware of.

→ **Don't soak a cast iron piece in soapy water** for more than a little while, as the soap will attack and erode the seasoning.

→ **Don't expose a hot-off-the-stove pan to cold water**—it can make the metal buckle.

→ **Never put cast iron in the dishwasher,** and never use soap meant for a dishwasher on cast iron—it's far too harsh.

→ **Don't use a metal scratch pad** to clean cast iron, unless you're removing layers of rust. For everyday cleaning, a nylon scrubber is best.

→ **Never throw away a cast iron piece,** even if it's coated with rust and a layer of char and grunge. Unless there are cracks in it, it can be rehabilitated.

STUDIES INDICATE THAT COOKING IN CAST IRON CAN ADD IRON TO YOUR FOOD. IF THIS IS A HEALTH CONCERN FOR YOU, YOU WILL WANT TO LIMIT OR AVOID FOODS COOKED THIS WAY.

What, exactly, is seasoning?

Cast iron is heavy and looks solid, but in fact has millions of tiny pores. When the pan heats and the metal expands, the pores expand as well. Seasoning occurs when oil gets into the pores and seals them, giving the pan a smooth invisible coating.

To season a new skillet,

griddle, Dutch oven, or any other piece of cast iron, wash in warm, sudsy water. Rinse thoroughly and dry completely. Using a paper towel, coat the entire utensil—inside, outside, and handle—with peanut oil. You don't want the oil dripping off the piece, but you do want a generous coating. Place in a 300°F oven for two or three hours, then remove from the oven and wipe off the excess oil with a paper towel. Do this several times before cooking with the pan. There's no such thing as one-session seasoning.

When you're ready to cook,

always preheat the pan for a few minutes over medium heat. At first, when a piece is still new, avoid cooking things that might undo the work that's been done.

No blackened fish, please! Also, avoid cooking acidic foods, such as tomatoes, as acid will also attack the seasoning. (Once the piece becomes well seasoned, this is not an issue.)

When the piece is still relatively new,

go out of your way to cook items that will reinforce the seasoning. In other words, anything that will involve grease or oil. Frying bacon is a good idea, as is sautéing. Don't turn the heat up too high, as that will also undermine your progress. It won't take long until you begin to notice that your skillet is cooking better, with little or no sticking.

Traditional advice warns against

using soap to clean cast iron. I confess I've never been able to forgo soap. Instead, I use mild dishwashing solution. After towel drying, I wipe the inside of the skillet with a paper towel with a small amount of oil on it, set the pan on a burner, and turn the flame on as low as I can get it for a minute or so. This was my mother's method, and worked so well for her I've followed suit.

To *reclaim a cast iron piece* that's got a lot of rust, scrub away as much of the rust as you can with a steel wool pad. Wash in warm soapy water and scrub some more while the piece is wet. Wash again and dry thoroughly. Repeat this as many times as it takes to remove all the rust, then re-season as described above.

You should re-season if you notice black bits of char on your dish towel or food has a metallic taste.

TAKING CARE OF TABLEWARE

If you store silverware in self-sealing plastic bags, it will tarnish much more slowly. Better yet, use your good silver daily. If you wash it by hand and dry it immediately, you can go for years without needing to polish it. A piece of chalk placed in your silver chest will also help prevent tarnishing, because it absorbs moisture.

Clean tarnished silverware with baking soda and hot water. Fill a kettle with water and bring to a boil. While it's heating, put an aluminum baking pan in your sink and spread the tarnished silverware in it. Sprinkle baking soda liberally over the silverware.

{ A small collection of salt and pepper shakers brighten this glass-fronted cabinet of stacked China. }

When the water comes to a boil, pour in enough to completely cover the silver. There will be a lot of bubbling and fizzing, but it's harmless. When all is quiet, check the pan—you'll see silver sparkling up at you. Repeat if necessary.

Hand wash vintage dishes and glasses, and be cautious about subjecting them to very hot water.

Waking up to a clean, bright kitchen is an easy way to start your morning right.

I don't know whether glass and china weren't tempered as well back then or whether they have become more fragile over time, but I've seen lovely pieces split in two when plunged into hot dishwater. To be safe, wash and rinse gently in warm water. The same goes for your good crystal glasses—the dishwasher can cause etching, fine scratches that make the glass look cloudy. Once etching has occurred, there is no remedy for it.

If crystal glasses are cloudy as a result of mineral deposits, you can get them clear again. First, try washing them in a gallon of water to which you've added a cup of white vinegar. If this doesn't do the trick, step it up a notch and soak them in the solution overnight. If the glasses are still cloudy, fill them with undiluted white vinegar and let them stand overnight. Use a non-scratching pad to wash them out in the morning.

To wash crystal, avoid plunging it in hot water—the sudden change in temperature may cause the glass to crack. Instead, dip the glass into the water sideways and let it warm gradually. Wash and rinse in warm water.

Avoid dried egg residue on dishes and plates by sprinkling salt on the egg right away when you stack the dishes. Even if it's several hours before they're washed, the egg will come off easily.

Round up stray glasses and dishes with a quick walk-through of the house before you do the day's last load of dishes.

KITCHEN ENERGY SAVERS

Refrigerators and freezers have become much more energy-efficient over the last decade. If yours date from the 1990s, you may actually save money by replacing them before they wear out.

Freezers run most efficiently when they're about 75 percent full. If your freezer doesn't have much in it, milk jugs filled with water are good stand-ins.

Set your refrigerators to 38-40°F and make sure they are full to capacity but not so crowded that air can't circulate.

If you have a larger refrigerator than you need, consider replacing it with a smaller model.

Cover all food in the fridge, especially liquids. Otherwise, the

TRY NOT TO OPEN THE OVEN DOOR WHEN YOU'RE BAKING OR ROASTING— THAT LITTLE PEEK CAN LET 20 PERCENT OF THE HEAT OUT.

moisture will cause the fridge to run longer.

Let hot foods cool naturally on the counter before putting them away.

Every three to six months, pull the refrigerator out and vacuum the coils at the back. Dust-clogged coils make the appliance work harder, using more energy.

Locate your fridge or freezer as far away as possible from hot-running items such as ovens and dishwashers.

Adding salt to the water you boil your food in will make the water boil hotter, reducing the amount of energy needed to cook the food.

Bake in glass or ceramic pans rather than metal ones, and you can reduce the oven temperature by 25°F.

When bringing large amounts of water to a boil, such as for pasta, keep the lid on—the water will come to a boil much more quickly.

Try cooking dishes simultaneously in the oven. Differences of up to 25 degrees can be made up for with adjustments in time, and won't affect the finished dish. If you have more items than will fit in the oven, try chain cooking, so the oven won't have to heat up all over again.

Clean your oven manually and only use the self-cleaning feature, which uses a significant amount of energy, when the job is major. When you do use it, conserve by starting while the oven is still hot from cooking something else.

The A-Z of Food

Where ordinary cooks gather, genius happens. To me, a few really good food tips are more valuable that a four-star chef's most treasured recipe. Here are some of my all-time favorites.

A

ADD A DASH

Sometimes even your favorite recipes need a little sprucing up. Next time you cook, try adding just a dash of:

✦ **Balsamic vinegar to spaghetti sauce:** Your sauce will taste like it's been simmering all day long.

✦ **Celery seed to barbecue sauce:** Celery seed adds a fresh

green note, even in a sauce that has been stored for weeks.

✦ **Cinnamon to chili:** The sweetness of cinnamon is a perfect counterpoint to hot chili spices.

✦ **Cocoa powder to rye bread dough:** Ever wonder how they get pumpernickel so dark? The secret is unsweetened cocoa powder, about two tablespoons per loaf. In addition to rich color, it gives the bread a nice bite as well.

✦ **Coffee to chocolate:** Coffee amplifies the taste of chocolate. Add a splash to cakes, brownies, and hot fudge sauce. The stronger the better—use espresso, if you have it.

✦ **Hot sauce to cheese sauce:** Cheese sauces and fondue can sometimes seem bland. Spark your taste buds with a few shakes of concentrated hot sauce. The same trick works with another rich favorite, guacamole.

✦ **Lemon juice to creamy spreads and dips:** Like cheese sauce, above, sour cream and cream cheese spreads, no matter how good they taste, can seem a bit too thick and rich. A good squirt of lemon juice brightens the taste and thins them just enough.

✦ **Mustard or horseradish to beef stew:** A spoonful of either of these will put some zing in your beef stew.

✦ **Nutmeg to muffin batter:** Nutmeg is the spice flavor in plain donuts, subtle yet delicious. Add a pinch to your favorite muffin recipe.

✦ **Oil to pasta water:** I never add salt to my pasta water, but I do add a few drops of oil. As a result, my pasta never clumps together or sticks to the bottom of the pot.

✦ **Paprika to flour:** If you're flouring pieces of chicken or steak to fry, add a generous dash of sweet paprika to the flour along with the salt and pepper. Depending on your tastes, experiment with other seasonings as well, such as onion salt, celery salt, and sage.

✦ **Salt to potato water:** Potatoes absorb more salt taste from the water they cook in than from salt added later on, so salting the water reduces your overall sodium intake.

ARTICHOKES

Unlike other fruits and vegetables, artichokes don't turn brown or develop spots as they pass their peak. Even as the flavor deteriorates, the appearance remains the same. What's a poor shopper to do? First, sneak a little squeeze. A fresh artichoke, which is actually a flower bud, will make a slight squeaking sound. It will also be compact and weighty. Pass up an artichoke that feels light for its size or whose petals are open. You can also gauge freshness by

130

examining the bit of stalk at the end. It should be firm to the touch and a good match in size. A stalk that is soft or thin was cut so long ago it's begun to dry out.

ASPARAGUS

To keep asparagus from turning dry and brown, treat it like freshly cut flowers. Trim the stalks an inch from the bottom, then stand them in a container tall enough to keep them from tipping over. Add about two inches of water, cover loosely with a plastic bag, and put them in the refrigerator. Add more water as necessary.

B

BEANS

One advantage of making baked beans, bean soup, and similar dishes from scratch is that you reduce the effect of the gas-producing legumes. Add a teaspoon of dried fennel seed to the water and your stomach will thank you.

BREAD

Not sure what to do with bread that's gone slightly stale or downright dry? Here are six ideas for using it up, from the least dry to hard as a rock.

✦ **French toast:** The French, who invented it, called it *pain perdu*—"lost bread"—a good name for a dish that uses bread that's too stale to be eaten. Fresh absorbs too much liquid to make good French toast, but bread a few days old—what a treat!

✦ **Bread pudding:** This delicious old-fashioned dessert can be made with everything from plain white bread to croissants to Hawaiian bread. It's a good way of using up stray bits of fruit as well—apples, bananas, figs, and dried fruit of all sorts go a long way when mixed with stale bread, custard, sugar, and spices.

✦ **Crostini:** If your stale bread is a baguette, slice very thin and toast the slices on a cookie sheet until completely crisp and golden brown. Crostini are less expensive than cocktail crackers, much more elegant, and the perfect platform for spreads and canapes. Stored in an airtight canister, they keep for months.

✦ *Croutons*: Toss cubes of stale bread in melted butter and olive oil (just enough to flavor and moisten slightly, not saturate) and season with herbs and spices as your mood commands. Celery seed, basil, oregano, onion, garlic, chili powder, turmeric, cumin—all can make you wonder why anyone would settle for store-bought.

✦ *Stuffing*: Dry bread broken into cubes is the backbone of classic stuffing, and the more kinds of bread in the mix—from yeast breads to quick breads and even sweet rolls—the better the finished product.

✦ *Bread crumbs*: There comes a day when bread is so rock hard large chunks are impossible to cut, cube, or break into pieces. When only a jackhammer will do, get out the food processor and make breadcrumbs. In addition to their role in meatball and meatloaf recipes, bread crumbs toasted in a skillet with a little melted butter and garlic seasoning are great sprinkled over casseroles and vegetable dishes.

BROWN SUGAR

Brown sugar that has hardened can easily be reclaimed. Place the hardened sugar in a container with an airtight lid. Thoroughly moisten a paper towel and squeeze out excess moisture. Make a small cup of aluminum foil and place the damp paper towel in it, place it in the container with the sugar, and secure the lid. In about an hour the sugar will begin to soften, and by tomorrow it will be as good as new.

BUTTER

If you buy unsalted butter (which, to my mind, tastes far better than salted), store sticks you don't plan to use right away in the freezer. Unsalted butter has no preservatives, and so has a shorter shelf life that salted butter.

CANAPÉ SPREAD

Canapé spread is made with eight ounces of cream cheese or Neufchâtel mixed with a stick of butter, and you should always have the ingredients on hand. With canapé spread, you can come up with an interesting snack spread at the drop of a hat. Good things to add are:

✦ Chopped green onions

✦ Grated cheddar, garlic, and a shot of Worcestershire or steak sauce

✦ Sliced black olives

✦ Sliced pimento-stuffed green olives and chili sauce

✦ Crumbled bacon and horseradish

✦ Chopped fresh vegetables

✦ Sautéed sweet red peppers and onions

✦ Sautéed mushrooms, fresh dill, and a squeeze of lemon juice

CANNED FOOD

Not all cans can be opened from the bottom, but it's worthwhile knowing which ones can. When you open a can from the bottom, food that usually settles and sticks will come out first, and you won't have to go after it with a spatula.

CARROTS

Raw carrots that have gone a bit limp can be revived if you mix a teaspoon of sugar with cold water, add the carrots, and chill them in the fridge for one to two hours. The same trick works with celery.

CELERY

Most people store celery in the plastic bag it came in. I've found it stays crisper and lasts longer if I discard the plastic bag and wrap it in aluminum foil. And while we're on the subject—don't discard the celery leaves. Add them to salads

or chop them up and sauté them with onions for spaghetti sauce, gravies, and other dishes.

CHEESE

Grating soft cheeses like mozzarella and Muenster can be a sticky, crumbly mess. For tidier cooking, put the cheese in the freezer for half an hour before you grate it.

CHILI

If you use ground beef in chili, try a mix of two-thirds ground beef and one-third pork sausage. The pork adds a tender, slightly sweet note that blends perfectly.

CUCUMBERS

Cucumbers seem to begin turning to mush almost as soon as they hit the vegetable bin. You can make them last longer by wrapping them tightly in plastic wrap. The same approach works for other high water content vegetables prone to mushiness, such as sweet peppers.

D

DESSERT

Don't panic when friends show up and you don't have dessert on hand—go to your fruit bowl. Fresh fruit is always elegant, and dresses for dinner beautifully. Here are some favorite combinations:

✦ Banana slices drizzled with a quick caramel sauce (butter and brown sugar melted together), topped with walnuts or pecans

✦ Cherries, pitted and simmered three to four minutes in a small amount of water and sugar (about three tablespoons of each per pound of fresh dark sweet cherries), and a squeeze of lemon, with brandy (about a quarter cup per pound) stirred in after removing from heat

✦ Orange slices with a dollop of sour cream

✦ Peaches and raspberries tossed with a sprinkle of powdered sugar and a splash of amaretto

◆ Pear slices sautéed in butter and brown sugar (this also works with apples, but pears are better)

◆ Strawberries and a splash of balsamic vinegar, strawberries with grated orange tossed in anise liqueur, or the classic strawberries and whipped cream

E

EGGPLANTS

This tip changed the way I feel about this little vegetable. I'd all but given up on buying them because so many seemed bitter rather than sweet and slightly smoky. A vendor at the local farmer's market told me what the problem was. Since it's the seeds that add the bitter taste, the trick is to buy male plants, because they have far fewer seeds than female ones. The way to tell which is which is to examine the large, rounded end. Males have a slight indentation, while females have a deeper, more pronounced indentation. If you look at enough eggplants, you'll soon be able to tell who's who.

EGGS

Everyone loves egg salad and deviled eggs, but peeling a hard-boiled egg is no picnic if you don't know how. First, choose older eggs to boil, because fresh eggs are the hardest to peel. As soon as the eggs have cooked, put them in cold water. When you're ready to peel them, gently crack the shells in several places. Hold the egg under cold running water, rolling it gently between your fingers to loosen the shell. Begin peeling at the large end, passing the egg under the water from time to time.

The shell should slip off without taking chunks of the white with it.

G

GARLIC

When choosing a head of garlic, give it a squeeze. It should be firm, and there should be no soft spots, browning sports, or missing skin. Missing cloves are fine, it just means you're buying less garlic. Reject any head that has sprouting cloves—the garlic has been in storage a long time, and sprouting drains the clove of its goodness. The same is true of onions—unless you're buying scallions, don't buy onions that have started to sprout.

GREEN TOMATOES

People seem to think the way to ripen green tomatoes is on a sunny windowsill. Well, no. Tomatoes ripen from the inside, and even if the skin reddens, the tomato underneath it won't be what you expected. Nothing substitutes for vine ripening, but the best method for ripening once they've come off the vine is to wrap them loosely in newspapers and put them in a dry, dark place at room temperature.

H

HAM

When your baked ham dwindles down to the last few slices and no one in the house can bear the thought of another ham sandwich, chop it into half-inch cubes. Chop some sweet red pepper and onion to go with it, bag the mix, and put it in the freezer. You may be tired of ham just now, but the day will come when a Western omelet sounds all but irresistible. Just shake some of the mix in a pan, sauté, and add eggs.

HAMBURGER

The secret to a truly juicy hamburger is not to pack the meat firmly. To shape, hold the burger-to-be in your palm, flatten the top lightly with your fingertips, then go around the edge, using your thumb to tap stray pieces into place. Instead of a leaden, meatball-dense burger, you'll have a light and tender delight.

- -

HERBS AND SPICES

- -

Have you become a little too reliant on salt, pepper, garlic, and onions? It's time to hit the spice rack and try some new flavorings. You probably already have most of these common herbs:

✦ Beef: allspice, basil, bay, caraway, cilantro, coriander, cumin, curry, dill, horseradish, lemongrass, marjoram, mustard, oregano, sage, tarragon, thyme

✦ Chicken: bay, basil caraway, coriander, cumin, dill, curry, ginger, lemongrass, marjoram, mustard, rosemary, sage, tarragon

✦ Duck: dill, ginger, lemongrass, rosemary, sage, tarragon

✦ Eggs: chives, dill, basil, chervil, coriander, cumin, curry, lemon balm, lovage, marjoram, mint, mustard, parsley, rosemary, sage, savories, tarragon, thyme

✦ Fish: anise, basil, caraway, chives, coriander, curry, dill, fennel, ginger, lemongrass, marjoram, parsley, rosemary, sage, tarragon, thyme

✦ Pork: allspice, anise, basil, chervil, cilantro, cinnamon, coriander, cumin, dill, fennel, ginger, lemongrass, marjoram, mustard, rosemary, sage, savories, tarragon, thyme

✦ Lamb: basil, bay, caraway, coriander, cumin, curry, dill, lemon balm, marjoram, mint, rosemary, sage, thyme

✦ Salads: anise, basil, caraway, chervil, chives, coriander, cumin, dill, edible flowers, lemongrass, parsley, tarragon, thyme

✦ Turkey: bay, basil, caraway, coriander, cumin, curry, dill, lemongrass, marjoram, mustard, rosemary, sage, tarragon, thyme

I

- -

ICED COFFEE

- -

If you love iced coffee on a summer's day, keep coffee ice cubes on hand. Made from freshly brewed coffee, they'll chill your drink without diluting it.

L

LETTUCE

Salad greens that have gone
a bit soggy can by revived by
soaking in cold water with some
lemon juice. To store, place in
a zip-style bag with a paper towel
to absorb moisture.

M

MASHED POTATOES

One of the secrets of good mashed
potatoes is boiling the potato until
it is soft enough to mash well,
but not so soft that it has become
waterlogged and flavorless. It's
a narrow window of opportunity,
and one I've missed many times.
One day at a farmer's market, I
lamented about this to a woman
I was buying heirloom potatoes
from. She told me to forget about
boiling the potatoes and try

steaming them instead. Although
this meant breaking with
thousands of years of tradition,
I was desperate enough to try it.
I've been steaming my mashing
potatoes ever since.

O

ONIONS

Onions that have been stored a
long time can become too strong
to enjoy. To take the edge off their
taste, slice and soak in cold water
for ten to fifteen minutes. Drain,
pat dry, and use as usual.

OVEN FRIES

For perfect oven fries from either
regular potatoes or sweet, soak
the peeled and sliced pieces in
very cold water for ten to fifteen
minutes. Drain well, pat dry, toss
with oil, season with salt and
pepper, then bake as usual.

P

PASTA

Keeping pasta hot until it gets to the table is easy: place a colander in the serving bowl and drain the pasta into it. Let it sit for about thirty seconds, then remove the colander, empty the bowl, and add the drained pasta.

PECANS

The easiest way to shell pecans is to freeze them in the shell.

This causes the nutmeat to pull away from the shell, and the shell to become slightly brittle. Shell them frozen and the nutmeat should come out without too much trouble.

POPCORN

Popcorn loses its popability when it dries out. For this reason, it's best not to store popcorn in the refrigerator or in self-defrosting freezers, as both tend to dry food out. For best storage, keep unpopped corn in airtight glass or plastic containers.

POTATOES

My grandfather was a master at growing potatoes, but it was my grandmother who knew how to store them and keep them tasty through the winter. I don't know all of her secrets, but one was to cut an apple in half and add it to the storage bin to keep them from sprouting. Another rule was never to store onions and potatoes together, as each would cause the other to spoil.

R

ROAST DUCK OR CHICKEN

Someone once told me I could make something very much like Peking duck if I let the bird sit, unwrapped, in my refrigerator for a few days before glazing and roasting it. Having made real Peking duck once, I laughed uproariously. But I tried it and the result was surprisingly crisp. Simply unwrap the birds, rinse inside the cavity and out, and pat dry. Set the duck on a rack in a roasting pan, breast side up, and leave it in the fridge for three days. When it's time to cook, rub with the glaze of your choice and roast as usual.

S

SUBSTITUTIONS

Don't drop everything and dash to the store when you're cooking and run out of something.

Chances are you have alternate ingredients on hand.

✦ *Baking powder:* 1 teaspoon baking powder = ½ teaspoon cream of tarter plus ¼ teaspoon baking soda

✦ *Brown sugar:* 1 cup brown sugar = 1 cup white sugar plus 2 tablespoons molasses

✦ *Butter:* ½ cup salted butter = ½ cup unsalted butter plus ¼ tsp salt. If you use salted butter in a recipe that should have unsalted butter, omit ¼ teaspoon salt called for per ½ cup of butter

✦ *Buttermilk:* 1 cup buttermilk = 1 teaspoon lemon juice (or vinegar) and enough milk to make one cup

✦ *Chocolate, semisweet:* 1 ounce semisweet chocolate = 3 tablespoons semisweet chocolate chips or 1 ounce unsweetened chocolate plus 1 tablespoon sugar

✦ *Chocolate, unsweetened:* 1 ounce unsweetened chocolate = 3 tablespoons unsweetened cocoa powder plus 1 tablespoon butter

✦ *Corn syrup, dark:* 1 cup dark corn syrup = ¾ light corn syrup plus ¼ cup molasses

✦ *Cornstarch:* 1 tablespoon cornstarch = 2 tablespoons flour

✦ *Flour, cake:* 1 cup cake flour = ¾ cup plus 2 tablespoons flour plus 2 tablespoons cornstarch, sifted together

SIMPLE COUNTRY WISDOM

+ **Flour, self-rising:** 2 cups self-rising flour = 2 cups flour plus 1 teaspoon baking soda plus 2 teaspoons baking powder plus 1 teaspoon salt

+ **Garlic:** 1 clove fresh garlic = ⅛ teaspoon garlic powder

+ **Garlic salt:** 1 teaspoon garlic salt = ⅛ teaspoon garlic powder plus enough salt to make 1 teaspoon

+ **Ginger:** 1 teaspoon fresh ginger = ¼ teaspoon powdered ginger

+ **Half-and-half:** 1 cup half-and-half = 1 tablespoon melted butter and enough whole milk to make 1 cup

+ **Herbs:** 1 tablespoon fresh herbs = 1 teaspoon dried herbs

+ **Lemon juice:** 1 teaspoon lemon juice = ¼ teaspoon cider vinegar

+ **Milk:** 1 cup whole milk = ½ cup evaporated milk plus ½ cup water

+ **Mustard, prepared:** ½ teaspoon ground mustard mixed with 2 teaspoons vinegar

+ **Onion:** 1 small, chopped onion = 1 teaspoon onion powder or 1 tablespoon dried minced onion

+ **Pumpkin pie spice:** 1 teaspoon pumpkin pie spice = ¼ teaspoon nutmeg plus ¼ teaspoon ginger plus ½ teaspoon cinnamon

+ **Sour cream:** 1 cup sour cream = 1 cup plain yogurt

+ **Sugar:** 1 cup sugar = 2 cups powdered sugar (Do not substitute in baking!)

+ **Tapioca:** 2 teaspooons tapioca = 1 tablespoon flour

T

TOMATOES

We all have happy visions of a pantry filled with home-canned tomatoes, but few of us have the same happy visions of standing in a hot, humid kitchen in July and August. Stay cool. Wash and core fresh tomatoes (skin them too, if you dislike the skins), then place in freezer containers or bags and freeze. Defrost at room temperature and enjoy your "canned" tomatoes.

TURKEY

There's no doubt that brining makes for juicier roast turkey and chicken, but it's also a bit of a nuisance. There's a much easier way to ensure juicy, flavorful roast fowl. Loosely stuff the cavity with quartered apples and stalks of celery. Their high water content will keep the bird moist, while their subtle flavors complement poultry perfectly.

TURKEY DAY LEFTOVERS

I love turkey and don't understand people who complain about Thanksgiving leftovers. One of my favorite dishes uses most of the foods used in the grand meal itself. To make it, press leftover bread stuffing into a quiche pan to form a crust. Chop leftover turkey and firm, cooked vegetables—such as carrots, broccoli, green beans, spinach, or leeks—into bite-sized pieces and set aside. (You should have two to three cups altogether.) Make a quiche base (four eggs per one cup half-and-half), add about a cup of grated cheese, and season with salt and pepper. Stir in the turkey and vegetables, pour into the prepared crust, and bake until firmly set.

WALNUTS

Love walnuts but get frustrated trying to get the meat out of the shell in whole pieces? Soak them overnight in salted water. (A teaspoon of salt will do.) The next day, drain and dry the walnuts on paper towels, and the meat will release in whole pieces when the nuts are cracked.

WILD RICE

I grew up in wild rice country and am amazed that so many people don't know what to do with it. First of all, wild rice is a grain, not a rice, so if you cook it plain, it's a bit ho-hum. Native Americans mixed it with wild blueberries and added it to venison stews, two ideas worthy of a four-star kitchen. I use it when I want a

quick, elegant side dish that goes with almost everything. To make it, chop some onion and bacon and sauté together until both are crisp.

Drain well and set aside. Cook the wild rice. Feel free to mix it with some white or brown rice if you want, just be sure to cook them separately, as they have different cooking times. Mix the bacon and onion with the rice and serve. A key feature of wild rice is that it's good hot, at room temperature, and even cold. So the next day, turn your leftovers into wild rice salad. Dress with a little lemon juice and oil and add whatever you have on hand. You can go sweet, adding ingredients such dried cranberries, blueberries, cherries, walnut, and pecans and dressing with a little orange juice; or you can go savory, adding sliced mushrooms, julienned carrots, and other raw vegetables and dressing with lemon vinaigrette. If you have leftover chicken, turkey, or duck, cut it in chunks or slivers and add it for a light, elegant main meal.

Better Living through Baking

I learned to bake years ago because, as a struggling writer, I could never afford to bring wine to dinner parties. I had to develop an alternative, and decided that homemade cakes, rolls, bread, and pies would do the trick. To this day, I feel a bit guilty about the accolades I received for commonplace items like cobblers and hot cross buns, while expensive bottles of wine were acknowledged with a shrug. The highlight of my efforts was a standing ovation from some Italian musicians who had come to America to give a concert. According to their translator, mine was the first "real" bread they'd had since landing in America. If you ever want to be extremely popular, with a full dance card and invitations as far as the eye can see, learn to bake.

I still bake at a moment's notice. In an overscheduled world, it's a wonderful stress reliever. It reminds me of what food is all about—the care that goes into its preparation, the beautiful alchemy of the ingredients, the warming aroma that has comforted mankind for thousands of years. Nothing signals "home" as clearly as the scent of baking bread, or makes me feel as optimistic about life as an apple pie cooling on the counter.

Baking is something I can do well and share with others, and it's healthy. A slice of homemade bread takes longer to eat and is far more satisfying than a slice of bread bought at the store. Pie isn't something that comes from a vending machine and gets washed down with soda. Cookies are a special treat somebody took the time to make. When you bake, you control what goes into your food. More raisins, less sugar. A pinch of salt instead of a tablespoon. Natural ingredients instead of preservatives. There are probably as many reasons to bake as there are bakers, and I hope everyone finds theirs somewhere along the way.

One final word: baking is not hard. Once you get the hang of it, it isn't even time consuming.

THE THREE COMMANDMENTS OF BAKING

Too many people think you can only get great baking results by using a special recipe or secret ingredient. Not at all! Good baking is no more complicated than doing the right thing at the right time. Here are a few simple guidelines to get you off on the right foot.

Bake often. The more frequently you bake, the more you will develop a feel for how dough should look and feel. In the old days, they called this having a "hand," referring to someone who knew by touch whether the bread had been kneaded enough, or if the pie crust would be flaky or tough. The more you develop your hand, the more chances you have to make corrections before your dish is baked. So it's important to bake often.

Accept mistakes. Baking has variables that aren't completely within your control. One year's crop of wheat may produce flour that's slightly lighter, or dryer, or denser than another year. The humidity in your house may be higher than usual or your baking powder may be losing its zest. Most of the time, these slight alterations don't matter but sometimes, for reasons you may never figure out, the forces of darkness conspire and you have a genuine failure on your hands. Shrug it off, it happens to everyone sometimes. Not all failures are bad, either. The most popular cookie of the twentieth century, the classic chocolate chip, began as a baking failure when the baker thought the chunks of chocolate she added would melt, mingle, and make an all-chocolate cookie.

Bake small. Many recipes got their start decades ago, when big families and big appetites

151

were the norm, and that "cooking big" style continues to dominate most contemporary cookbooks. Large quantity results can seem daunting, and wasteful, especially since most baked goods are best eaten when the bloom of freshness is still on them. Fortunately, most recipes can be divided. I divide recipes all the time, and divide them again. A deep dish pie, with fruit that needs to be peeled and large top and bottom crusts that need to be mixed and rolled out, is a major undertaking—so major, I don't do it often. But I will make any number of pies in my small-sized pie pan, using up stray handfuls of fruit, turning a left-over egg white into meringue topping, and combining leftover bits of ham and cheese into a perfect quiche for two.

{ Use large eggs for baking, not extra large or jumbo. Recipes are written and tested with Grade A large eggs, and using larger or smaller eggs than called for will throw your recipe off. }

BETTER BAKING

Read the instructions. Then reread them. It's amazing how many people—including myself—either skip the directions because they feel the item is one they already know how to make, or read the directions and get something wrong. There was once a banana cake recipe I loved the taste of and made for years, even though it repeatedly came out dense and flat. One day, flipping through the cookbook, I noticed that the two eggs I'd been adding should have been separated, and the whites beaten before adding. The cake was even better—not to mention higher and lighter—the next time I made it.

Have ingredients at room temperature. Eggs produce better volume at room temperature, and butter creams more easily. If your kitchen is very warm, you want butter slightly cooler than true room temperature, as you don't want the oils to begin to separate from the solids.

Use unsalted butter. Most recipes call for salt, and the

Frost your cupcakes the night before serving for a bakery-perfect look.

amount rests on the assumption that the butter used doesn't contain any. In addition to keeping your cooking accurate, unsalted butter tastes better—fresher because it has no preservatives and salt is not covering up its natural sweetness.

Should you sift? If flour seldom has the clumps and occasional stray husks that flour of long ago did, why are we still sifting? Well, there's another reason why sifting is important. You also may have noticed that directions usually say "sift the dry ingredients together." This is because you don't want to beat flour longer than necessary. When you make bread, you want to work and knead the flour to develop the glutens. But for other baked goods, such as pies, cakes, and cookies, working the flour will make pastry tough rather than tender. On the other hand, leavenings and spices, which are added in relatively small amounts, have to be thoroughly blended into the dough. Sifting dry ingredients together is a good way to get the job done without having to beat the flour. You can cheat; instead of sifting, measure the ingredients into a bowl and stir well with a fork.

Give your oven enough time to preheat, at least ten and preferably fifteen minutes.

Ovens don't bake alike. Smaller ovens seem to bake more quickly, while older ovens can develop hot spots and cool spots. The first time you use a recipe that involves baking, watch it like a hawk. Note the time when you slid the pan into the oven, and make a notice of when you take it out. That's the true baking time, the one that works for your oven, and it may be different from what the recipe says.

Oven thermometers are great, but many people make the mistake of hanging the gauge on the front of the rack where it's easiest to read. The problem is that you don't bake food at the very front of your oven, where the temperature is the coolest. Hang the thermometer in the center of the oven, where the food will go.

No peeking. Every time you open your oven door, you lose at least 25 degrees of heat. This not only wastes energy, it will throw your times way off and, in some items, will affect the quality of the finished product.

LEAVE YOUR OVEN LIGHT OFF DURING THE BAKING PROCESS. IT ADDS HEAT, BUT ADDS IT UNEVENLY, AT THE BACK OF THE OVEN, WHICH IS ALREADY HOTTER THAN THE FRONT OF THE OVEN.

a.m. - pick up dahlias
from flower ranch
p.m. - coffee + goodies!

TIPS FOR BAKING POWDER BISCUITS

For extra-flaky biscuits, use frozen butter for the shortening, and grate it into the flour or pulse in a food processor.

My mother rolled her biscuits out and used a cutter. I seldom have time for that, and simply pat my dough into a rectangle and cut the biscuits into squares. You can also turn the dough out onto a sheet and pat it into a large circle. Using the dull side of a knife blade, score the dough into pie-shaped wedges. Bake, and cut apart when the biscuits are done.

A well-seasoned cast iron skillet makes a perfect pan to bake biscuits in. Melt a tablespoon or so of butter in it, tilt the pan so that the entire bottom is coated, add biscuits and bake.

Before you put your biscuits in the oven, sprinkle them with salt and pepper. This tastes especially good if you're serving them with a mild, rich dish such as clam chowder or oyster stew.

THE PERFECT LOAF OF BREAD

Bread is far easier to make than many things you already cook. If you lack confidence, go to the library, find the books on making bread, and take a few home with you. Browsing through them, you'll notice that every recipe has four basic ingredients: leavening (usually yeast, but sometimes a starter), water, flour, and salt. While there are differences from one recipe to the next—different proportions, different mixing methods, different added ingredients—the basic four are always there, and so long as you don't kill the yeast, and give the chemistry time to work, you will end up with bread.

Once you've mastered pizza crust, branch out to other

PIZZA CRUST IS A GOOD PLACE TO START BECAUSE YOU DON'T HAVE TO WORRY ABOUT IT RISING, AND EVEN IF IT'S NOT QUITE PERFECT, NO ONE WILL NOTICE ALL THAT MUCH.

flatbreads, such as focaccia, fougasse, naan, lavash, or pita. Since some flatbreads are yeast-risen and some aren't, it will give you a good feel for the two types of dough.

Don't use fast-rising yeast.
Some people get into such a dither about their bread not rising they take out "yeast insurance"—they buy rapid-rise yeast, or try to give the yeast a boost by using self-rising flour with it, or use regular yeast but throw in an extra spoonful for good measure. All of these are bad ideas. The salt in the self-rising flour is antagonistic to yeast, and will slow down or limit its effectiveness. At the other end of the spectrum, the satisfying taste and texture of bread comes from giving the gluten time to develop, and while fast-rising yeast can produce a lot of bubbles, it can't really speed up time.

Use good water.
Water is one of the dominant flavorings in bread. If the tap water in your area has a lot of chlorine, or doesn't taste good for other reasons, use good bottled water.

Use good flour.
White flour is the backbone of most breads—even rye breads and wheat breads. Everyone who bakes has a favorite type. Mine is unbleached, and I can't imagine switching my allegiance. Others I know use bleached flour, while still others want to see the words "Bread Flour" on the sack. All of these are good flours, and they're all available in the grocery story. Experiment to see which you like best—as long as you avoid cake flour and self-rising flour, you'll be fine. Health food stores are also good places to explore, and you'll find greater variety, too—semolina flour, organically grown flour, and stone-ground white flour are just some of the types I've found there.

Mix bread in the largest bowl you have.
In the old days, people mixed dough in wide, shallow wooden bowls. This shape, larger than needed to hold the ingredients, meant that a lot of air got mixed in right from the start. You can get the same advantage by using a bowl that doesn't crowd ingredients to the brim, and is shallow enough to let air circulate freely.

Don't add flour all at once.
Instead, add about half a cup at a time and beat after each addition. This is another way of lightening the dough.

Most recipes tell you to turn the finished dough
onto the counter and let it rest ten minutes before kneading. I've had

A WAY TO GET SHINY, CRUSTY LOAVES IS TO MIST THE BREAD WITH A SPRAY MISTER SEVERAL TIMES WHILE IT'S BAKING, ONCE EVERY TEN TO FIFTEEN MINUTES.

better luck another way. I turn the dough onto the board when it's still sticky, and work in the last of the flour with my hands. Then I knead it for a few minutes, put a cloth over it, and let it rest fifteen to twenty minutes. When I come back and begin the "real" kneading, I find that the longer resting period, and the little bit of kneading I did before, makes my job a lot easier.

Another trick that makes for more efficient kneading is to delay adding the salt. Don't add it to the dough while you're mixing, but hold back until halfway through the kneading process.

The most common error in breadmaking comes during the kneading process. It's easy to decide the dough is too sticky, and start adding more and more flour to correct the problem. The problem is that too much flour gets added, and added so late in the process that the bread becomes leaden. I learned all this the hard way. Ultimately, I learned to resist the impulse to keep adding more flour—kneading will usually take care of the stickiness, it just takes some time.

If you want a crusty, artisan-style loaf, try adding less yeast and slowing down the rising time. A general rule of thumb is that cutting the yeast in half will double the rising time.

Rotate the bread halfway through baking, to make sure it bakes evenly.

Deciding when bread is done baking can be tricky, since no two loaves are ever quite the same. The foolproof way is to buy an instant read thermometer to check the bread's internal temperature. Sandwich breads, which you want to be slightly moist, are done when the internal temperature hits 180°F. Breads that you want to be crisper and dryer, such as baguettes, are done at 200°F.

Always let bread cool on a rack, to keep the bottom crisp, and don't try to slice it until it's cooled considerably.

When the bread is still warm but cool enough to cut, be sure to enjoy a slice. Fresh bread with butter or a slice of sharp cheddar is about as close to nirvana as you can get.

CAKES AND MORE

Boxed mix cakes have given us the idea there are only a handful of flavors and frostings. Go find a vintage cookbook and you'll see how far off the mark this is. Back in the days when people

baked from scratch, there were dozens and dozens of flavors and combinations. You'll find enough inspiration to keep you going for years.

To bake a perfect cake, get off on the right foot—make sure all ingredients are at room temperature.

Don't skimp on the time you spend creaming the butter and sugar—this is how the air that makes cake light gets incorporated into the batter. Cream the butter on its own for about five minutes, then add the sugar and cream until the mixture is no longer gritty.

Combine the cake's dry ingredients in a bowl and stir well, using a fork to fluff and lighten the flour.

When adding dry ingredients, don't beat. Mix in at medium speed, and don't mix longer than necessary to blend thoroughly.

If you use butter or margarine in the cake, use the wrapper to grease the cake pan. It has just about the right amount of shortening clinging to it.

If you don't want to grease or flour the cake pan, line the

USE THE FRESHEST EGGS AVAILABLE FOR YOUR CAKES. THE FRESH ONES PRODUCE MORE VOLUME WHEN BEATEN.

TO MAKE YOUR CHOCOLATE CAKE MOISTER, MIX THE BAKING SODA WITH A TEASPOON OF VINEGAR BEFORE ADDING.

bottom of the pan with waxed paper or baking parchment and leave the sides bare—the cake can be loosened by running a spatula along the edges.

Chocolate cakes can pick up white streaks from the flour that coated the pan. To avoid this, dust the pan with cocoa powder instead.

Look for a recipe with buttermilk in it for a cake that will stay moist a long time. Keep the cake in the refrigerator, well wrapped, and it will last for weeks.

When it's time to frost the cake, decide what kind of look you want. For a casual, rustic look, stack the layers right side up. For a bakery shop look, trim the domes off each layer and invert them.

Another plus: the buttermilk adds a richness that makes frosting unnecessary. A dusting of powdered sugar, simple glaze, or dollop of frosting is all that's needed.

Rap the filled pan sharply on the counter a few times before putting your cake in the oven, to bring the air bubbles to the surface.

To bake a cake that's more level than domed, use the back of a large spoon to pull batter from the center out towards the edges.

Always make plenty of frosting. You can freeze the leftovers, or spread it on graham crackers for a special treat.

Before frosting a layer cake, go over the layers lightly with a pastry brush to sweep away loose crumbs.

To frost a cake on the plate you plan to serve it on, cut wide strips of baking parchment and arrange them to form a square covering the edges of the plate.

Put a dollop of frosting at the center of the cake plate and spread it out. This will anchor the cake and keep it from sliding around when you work at it.

FROSTING TO PERFECTION

To frost a two-layer cake, follow this order:

1 **First, the bottom layer.** Spread the filling or frosting evenly, right up to the edge. Add the top layer. If the frosting is a bit runny, pop the cake in the fridge for about ten minutes.

2 **Mix about one-third cup of frosting** with a few drops of milk, and spread a thin coat of frosting over the cake, sides first, then top. Return the cake to the refrigerator for ten to fifteen minutes, until the undercoat has set.

3 **Now finish the cake** with the remainder of the undiluted frosting, beginning with the sides. Make sure there is plenty of frosting on the spatula at all times, so that it glides smoothly over the cake and doesn't tug or tear at it. When reloading the spatula, wipe the excess off on the edge of the bowl, then wipe the spatula clean before reloading.

4 **Do the top last.** Plop a generous amount of frosting in the center of the cake and spread outward to the sides.

Give yourself room to spread out when you are baking. Clear the countertops or use an island.

If you want your frosted cake to have a smooth, shiny bakery look, hold a flat metal spatula under hot running water. Shake off the moisture or wipe lightly, but leave it a bit damp. Glide the spatula of the sides and top of the cake, re-heating as necessary, until the whole cake is smooth.

TRICKS FOR CHEESECAKES

Place a pan of water on the rack below the cheesecake. Your cake will be particularly moist and creamy.

Make sure all the lumps are out of the cream cheese when mixing a cheesecake, before you begin adding the eggs. Keep the mixer set at medium throughout— not high. The reason is that you don't want to beat air into the batter. You want a smooth, dense cake, not a light and frothy one.

A cheesecake is done when an inserted knife comes out slick but with just a bit of cake clinging to it. If batter is clinging to the whole knife, it isn't done yet. If you wait until the knife comes out completely clean and dry, you've baked the cake too long.

If your cake cracks on top when you want it to look perfect, don't despair. Pull it out of the oven as soon as you notice and set aside. Mix a cup of sour cream with one-quarter cup of sugar and a teaspoon of vanilla. When the cheesecake has cooled just enough to avoid melting the sour cream, spread the mixture evenly over the top and bake another fifteen to twenty minutes at 325°F. You'll have a picture perfect—and delicious—cake.

If you fear you've overbaked your cheesecake, don't despair. Let it cool, remove the springform ring, wrap the cake in plastic wrap, and put in the refrigerator. By serving time, the cake will not seem overbaked at all. The plastic wrap remoisturizes the cake, and any toughening that occurred vanishes.

Try replacing half the vanilla with pure almond extract for a subtle variation.

No springform pan? No worry. Any sturdy, straight-sided

TEA WITH A LEMON SLICE IS A PERFECT COMPANION TO A SWEET CHERRY PIE. TRY A TOP CRUST THAT IS SLIGHTLY TOO SMALL FOR A RED RING.

ovenproof dish will do. I have a six-inch soufflé dish I use when I want to make a small cake. The first time I did this, I wasn't quite certain how I'd get the cake out. I lightly buttered the dish, and when the cake was finished, I flipped it out onto a serving plate. I was going to flip it to another plate to get it right side up, but it was a chocolate cheesecake and I liked the way it looked, so I served it as is. The cake was a success, and the crust stayed nice and crisp until the last piece was eaten several days later.

QUICK COBBLERS AND MORE

It's hard to find a dessert as delicious—or as easy—as fruit cobbler. My mother used to roll out her dough for the top, but I prefer dropping mine over the fruit by large spoonfuls. It's much quicker, and the unevenness of the dollops makes delicious peaks and valleys to catch cream that's poured over the top as a finishing touch.

Some of my favorite cobblers are made from soft fruits—such as berries and peaches—that can collapse and become almost unrecognizable during baking. I solved this problem by using frozen fruit, tossing the ice-cold, rock-solid berries or peaches in a mix of cornstarch and sugar, getting the topping on quickly, and popping the whole thing in the oven as fast as possible. This way, the fruit spends much of the baking time thawing out, with less time to turn to jam.

BAKE COOKIES ANYTIME

Be the lady with the freshly baked cookies—anytime. Almost any cookie dough will work as slice-and-bake. Slit the cardboard core of a roll of paper towels or aluminum foil lengthwise and line with a piece of plastic wrap. Holding the core open, spoon in cookie dough, pressing firmly with a spoon to eliminate air pockets. Squeeze the tube together, scraping off any dough that oozes out. Wrap the excess plastic wrap around the tube, folding over the ends, then store in a plastic bag in the back of the freezer. When company drops by, just slice and bake as many cookies as desired. Keep a few different kinds of dough around, and treat your friends to a real cookie fest.

DON'T USE COOKIE SHEETS THAT GO WALL-TO-WALL IN YOUR OVEN. YOU NEED SPACE ON ALL FOUR SIDES IN ORDER FOR AIR TO CIRCULATE PROPERLY—ABOUT TWO INCHES ON EACH SIDE IS RECOMMENDED.

When bringing butter to room temperature for cookies, don't let it sit too long. Butter that is too soft makes batter that is too soft, and your cookies won't be crisp.

When recipes call for creaming butter, sugar, and eggs until light and fluffy, they mean it. Many people mix just to combine, then add the dry ingredients and beat much longer, at a higher speed. This is exactly backwards. "Light and fluffy" should get the lion's share of time, until the mixture has increased in volume and looks smooth and almost frosting-like. Then lower the speed and mix in the pre-sifted dry ingredients just until thoroughly combined. Beating dry ingredients for prolonged periods is where the phrase "tough cookies" originated.

Insulated cookie sheets produce great cookies with fewer burned edges and bottoms. If you don't have an insulated sheet, improvise by placing one cookie sheet on top of another.

Try to avoid greasing your cookie sheets. Greasing with butter can make cookies brown too quickly, while margarine or sprays can leave a taste. Invest in a silicon mat to put on the sheet, use baking parchment, or try a nonstick sheet.

Be sure your oven is fully heated when you put the cookies in. If it isn't, your cookies will be too flat, and even slightly greasy to the touch.

Ovens are hotter at the back than the front, where the door is. Halfway through the baking time, reverse the pan for thoroughly even baking. The longer the baking time is, the more important this step becomes.

As soon as cookies are cool enough to slide onto a spatula without breaking, transfer them to a wire rack to cool. Cookies that cool in the pan will not have crisp bottoms.

Either let your baking sheets cool between batches or, if possible, use two different cookie sheets. Shortening has a low melting temperature, so placing cookie dough on a warm baking sheet causes it to melt and ooze out of the dough. You want to keep the shortening in the dough where it belongs. If you don't have two baking sheets and are making drop cookies with medium to stiff dough, you can form the drops on a plate. Then, quickly transfer them to the baking sheet when it's free. Work fast and all should be well.

Burned cookies? Let them cool completely, then try using a small grater to gently remove the burnt edges and bottoms.

PIE CRUST

You will *never* get flaky, tender, old-fashioned pie crust with butter or oil. You must use lard. And before you wrinkle your nose up at the idea, know the facts: when compared to butter, lard has less cholesterol, less saturated fat, and a greater proportion of unsaturated fats.

Forget the pastry blender. To cut shortening into flour, put the ingredients in a food processor and pulse to the desired consistency.

Avoid the "chilled pastry dough" pitfall. Yes, chilling re-solidifies the shortening and makes for flakier crust, but many people think this means the dough should be chilled before it gets rolled out. This is a misconception, and chilling dough before you roll it will only give you a stiff mass that you will have to overwork to roll out. Roll the bottom crust out first and put it in the pan, then chill it in the pan. Then roll the top crust out on a piece of waxed paper, slide the paper onto a baking sheet or plate, and put it in the fridge. Or better yet, use lard as suggested above and your crust will be flaky without chilling.

Handle the dough as little as possible. If the piece is uneven or splits during rolling, it's better to do patchwork repair in the pan than to roll it out a second time. Rolling it out a second time will toughen the crust.

If you have trouble rolling out pie crust, try rolling it out between two sheets of waxed paper. When it's the right size, carefully peel one sheet of the paper away, flip the crust into the pie plate, and gently peel away the remaining sheet of paper.

When you flute the edges of the dough, remember that this isn't just for decoration. You really want to seal the top and bottom crusts together to keep juices from trickling out during baking, so give them a good pinch.

If your crust turns out soggy when you make fruit pies or pumpkin pie, try partially pre-baking them. About ten minutes at 350°F should do.

Don't throw leftover scraps of pie crust away. Cut them into cookie-sized pieces and bake until golden brown. Sprinkle with sea salt and eat plain, or skip the salt and eat topped with a slice of fresh peach or a dollop of raspberry jam.

QUICHE MAKES LEFTOVERS FUN

Quiche is wonderful for turning leftovers into delicious meals. Start with a good basic egg-and-dairy mix (four eggs per one cup of half-and-half works well for a nine-inch quiche) and add combinations of meat, cheeses, and cooked vegetables. Good combinations include:

- ✦ Artichokes and pecorino or Romano cheese
- ✦ Corn, bacon, and cheddar
- ✦ Ham and blue cheese
- ✦ Peppers, onions, and mushrooms, sautéed together
- ✦ Spicy sausage and sautéed peppers
- ✦ Spinach and feta or Gruyère cheese
- ✦ Turkey, bacon, and broccoli
- ✦ Zucchini and mozzarella cheese

If you don't have half-and-half on hand when you want to make quiche, and still want something richer than milk, canned evaporated milk is a perfect substitute.

HARMONY

9

In the Garden

···············— — — — — — —···············

Country gardens conjure up images of tree swings and tellises, hollyhocks and pole beans, vine-ripened tomatoes and dewy grass tickling sleepy bare feet. It's a user-friendly setting, perfect for quiet afternoons in a shaded hammock, boisterous holiday celebrations, and easy-living family suppers at the picnic table. Even if a busy schedule leaves little time for a full-blown vegetable patch, wildflower gardens, ivy, and shrubs are low-maintenance alternatives. Whether we have an acre to call our own or no more than a window box, the pleasures of getting one's fingers in the wet earth and seeing what comes up has an irresistible pull.

A BIG BOUQUET OF ALL-PURPOSE TIPS

A house starts inviting you in before you have even fully approached the front gate. Keep a neat, trim yard with at least a few flowers to welcome guests, and beware of overgrown landscaping that buries your house in so much gloom the

neighborhood kids start referring to it as "the scary witch house."

Protect your home from winter blasts and drifting snow by sheltering the exposed side of your house with a windbreak of trees and shrubs. For best results, the distance between the windbreak and the house should be two to five times the height of the mature plants, but distances double or even triple this can still produce results. Expect to save 25 percent on heating costs in ordinary conditions, and savings up to one-third in windy areas. Windbreaks on three sides (west, north, and east) can cut heating costs by as much as 40 percent. When choosing plants, consider those with low, bushy crowns and trees that will still give shelter in the winter.

If you can't create a windbreak, you can still use outdoor plantings to make the indoors comfortable. Shrubs, bushes, and vines planted near the house help maintain indoor temperatures in both summer and winter by creating pockets of dead air that act as insulation. Space the plants so that, when fully grown, there will be at least a foot of space between them and the exterior wall.

Draw a scale grid of your yard—front, back, and sides. Draw in anything that's truly permanent—the house, driveway, and any detached buildings. Save the original and make several copies—you'll always have a handy canvas to try new layouts on.

Be bold when you lay out your garden, and don't just settle for border plantings that hug the house or fencing. One of the most charming gardens I was ever in belonged to my sister's neighbor, who'd treated the space the same way you'd treat a living space. There was a winding stone walk that led to a conversation area with two bright yellow chairs, an area near the house for outdoor dining, a spot sheltered from these "people places" for a bird and butterfly garden, and farthest away from all of these a place for sports and recreation.

To make a shallow yard seem larger, use horizontal layers of different heights to create the illusion of depth, such as low shrubs before a slightly higher fence, flower beds and an arbor beyond, and taller shrubs near the house.

If you're good at computer imaging, take exterior shots of your home, enlarge them, and use an imaging program to paste or paint in various plantings you're contemplating.

Keep ground plans, notes, and inspiration pictures together in a garden workbook. Note your plantings for each season, how well they produced, and any problems you had along the way. Over just a few years, you'll build

A WAY TO MAKE A YARD OR GARDEN APPEAR BIGGER IS TO OPT FOR CURVING PATHS AND WALKWAYS RATHER THAN STRAIGHT ONES.

Carve out a sitting spot in your garden.
What's the point in having a beautiful yard
if you can't enjoy it?

a remarkably rich resource book—and you'll have your own personal wish book to get you through those long winter nights.

Keep a garden calendar. If
you plant from seed, it's especially useful to note your planting day and the day seedlings first appeared. (The wait always seems longer than it is, and I convince myself the plants should be up sooner than is realistic.) It's also helpful to note which days it rained and the amount of rainfall, so you don't water unless you really need to. Saving your calendars from year to year can give you a good record of conditions in your area, so I note once-a-season events such as the first killing frost, winter precipitation, and spring warming.

Fill a basket or caddy with all your tools you'll need, so you
won't have to keep gong back and forth and searching for the trowel or rake you just know is in the garage somewhere.

If the shade at the base of a
tree is too heavy for anything to grow there, try filling the bare ring with red mulch. It looks tidy and adds a bit of natural color.

Lawn not living up to its potential as an emerald beauty?
The two most common issues are the wrong soil and the wrong cutting. Fortunately, both can be corrected. Have your soil tested to make sure it's sufficient in iron and magnesium, the nutrients chiefly responsible for grass's rich green color. It's a common problem, and fertilizers tailored to correct the deficiency are available at your local garden shop. If soil isn't the problem, chances are you're cutting your lawn too short and too often, and the sun is taking its toll on those tender shoots. Grass should not be cut shorter than two inches, which means you've got some time to kick back and have an iced tea on the deck.

It's better to give your lawn
and plants a good soaking less frequently than several sprinklings more often. The reason is that the roots, the only part of the plant that can really absorb the water, lie underneath the soil. Small waterings are quickly absorbed by the topsoil, or even the matting of plant material that covers it, and the roots remain dry and thirsty. For them to drink, the water really has to penetrate—about four to

DON'T PRUNE ON A WINDY DAY. THE STIFF BREEZE CAN DRY THE TIPS OF THE BRANCHES, WHICH HAVEN'T YET HAD TIME TO FORM A PROTECTIVE SEAL.

six inches down for most lawns and plants, more for larger plants and shrubs.

Lawns need about an inch of water a week, although this can vary depending on factors such as cloud cover, air temperature, and humidity. A rain gauge helps you keep track of natural rainfall, but how do you know how much water your sprinklers put out? The answer is to do a test using the rain-gauge model. Mark an empty tin can one inch from the bottom and set it in a level, stable place in the sprinkler's range. Make note of the time and turn on the sprinkler. Keep watch on the can, and when the water reaches the one-inch marker, note the time again. The difference is how long you need to water each section of lawn a week.

I tried planting in the rain after reading a book about Russian peasants waxing nostalgic for the good old days and would recommend the experience to everyone. The pleasure of getting completely wet and muddy, the extra-sharp scent of greenery and damp earth, and the feeling of being completely in nature's grasp is not to be missed. And when it's over, the greatest pleasure of all awaits— there is nothing that feels as good as a long hot shower when you are chilly and soaked to the skin.

When starting seedlings in flats, add a little fertilizer to their water when the plants begin to appear. This will strengthen and fortify them for transplanting.

Save your small plastic yogurt containers and cut the bottoms—they're perfect for protecting seedlings from spring weather.

For those who prefer the inefficient way to clean up fallen leaves: rake them into lines in the shape of a floor plan for a small house with a few rooms. Don't forget the doors! Now your young ones can play while you finish raking, and you won't have to worry about them wandering off. Don't be surprised if you're invited for tea and graham crackers.

Don't transplant on a bright sunny day. Wait for early dusk or a cloudy day, so the plants won't dry out. Since moisture is a key to successful transplanting, I like to do it when the soil is still damp from rain. Even when that's the case, new transplants need to be

{ The efficient way to clean up fallen leaves is to rake them into a pile, then soak the pile with a garden hose on high pressure. Once they're wet they clump together and won't blow around, making it easy to transfer them to a mulch pile or shovel them into trash bags. }

watered immediately, to keep the roots from drying and withering. To be safe, water each plant as you go along.

If you have a working fireplace, mix the ashes with clean, dry leaves and let the leaves decompose. You will have an excellent leaf mold.

What to do with that pile of soot from cleaning your furnace pipes or chimney? Blend it into the soil around roses and lilies and it will deepen their color.

Many folks who want a hotbed but think it's too much work are ignoring an almost ready-made opportunity in their own backyards. It isn't difficult to build a hotbed frame that sits flush against a basement window. When the weather is bad you can pull up a stepladder and garden from the inside, and when it turns cold, leaving the window cracked open will let heat flow into the bed. The best side to build on is the south, but east will also work— these are the sides that get the most natural heat and light.

Garden tools get dull— especially the ones that prune bark-covered branches and hack through tough, fibrous roots—so sharpen the blades from time to time. An ordinary mill file, available at any hardware or home improvement store, is all you need.

Wash and dry your tools after each gardening session. Dirt left on blades turns into something much like cement, and if the earth is damp, rust may form.

Before putting lawn tools away for the winter, perform a maintenance check and inventory of all the items. Wash and thoroughly dry each tool. Check wooden-handled ones and sand away any splinters. Finally, give the clean, dry metal parts a good wipe with a cloth dipped in any kind of fat or oil, including ordinary salad oil or bacon fat left from breakfast—it will keep rust from forming.

Gardening question you can't find the answer to? Tap into any of the many extension services attached to public colleges and universities. They're an excellent source of information,

and the ones in your area can give you invaluable pointers on the soil, climate, and growing conditions in your region. Don't discount farther-flung branches, though—most specialize in locally grown crops. I know from personal experience that the Universities of Minnesota and Washington know about all there is to know about apples, and I bet the folks in Vermont could tell me a lot about harvesting sap for maple syrup.

ATTRACTING BIRDS AND BUTTERFLIES

We've all had dreams of a garden space alive with rainbow-colored butterfly wings and the spirit-lifting chirp of birds. But does your weed- and insect-free yard, with its scrupulously pruned trees, dead-headed flowers, and wide stretches of close-cropped grass, keep getting the cold shoulder? No wonder—to birds and butterflies this "perfect" landscape is as inviting as a picnic on the moon. There's nothing to eat here, no place to rest, and no protection from weather and predators. Here are some ways to put out the welcome mat without compromising too many of your aesthetic ideals.

Do the research. Find out how the birds and butterflies in your locality thrive. What kind of landscape and plants do they like to live near? Nature walks can give you some good insights, and your local nursery might also help, but we've found extension services (run by state universities and local governments) to be the most abundant source of information.

Start an inventory. In the wild, birds and butterflies live in habitats that are multitiered, among a diverse assortment of plants that provide for their needs throughout the seasons. Assess your space and start taking notes. Does your yard provide some "prairie," some "woods," and some border areas in between? Is there food and shelter throughout the seasons? Keep taking notes as you build your knowledge, and use them as a guide to make gradual changes over the course of several planting seasons.

Shun chemicals. Look into natural ways to control pests and weeds. (See Natural Pest Control, page 198). Not only can chemicals do harm when ingested, they are often indiscriminate killers, wiping out helpful insects along with pests. Increasing the number of plants native to your area is a good step, since they've already developed a resistance to local fauna, but your biggest asset is the creatures you're trying to attract—birds thrive on insects and worms, so let them do their part.

Food first. Butterflies enjoy fruit, drawing off the juice that's in it. For them, juicy, overripe offerings work best, placed well away from the bird feeder and at flower to shoulder height. Your local garden store will have good seed mixes for the birds in your area, but don't stop there. Birds also enjoy fruit such as berries, cherries, apples, peaches, plums, and grapes, while suet and peanut butter provide vitally needed extra fat for winter birds. Scatter some millet or cracked corn on the ground near the feeders in winter as well, for ground-feeders like sparrows and cardinals.

Choose a spot for your feeder that's visible from indoors, so you can enjoy the comings and goings, but where birds won't be unsettled by house traffic, noise, or prowling pets. Because birds need to feel secure when they feed, an ideal spot offers them an unobstructed view and is within six to ten feet of a tree or other high perch, in case a quick escape is needed. Remember that some species will only feed from the

ground, so when filling your feeder, scatter a fair amount of seed on the ground as well. If possible, locate more than one feeder in your yard, as some species are territorial and will not share space with others.

Add to the supply of food that attract birds by planting species that provide nuts, seeds, and fruit throughout the year. Not all of these are obvious—juniper berries may not interest us, but birds love them, while the evergreen cones we think of as lawn debris are rich in nutritious seeds. Here's a list of birds and trees they find especially appealing, either because the produce food or provide shelter.

- ✦ **American goldfinch:** birch, eastern hemlock
- ✦ **Bluebird:** red cedar
- ✦ **Chickadee:** butternut, white pine
- ✦ **Grosbeak:** balsam fir, crab apple, eastern hemlock, maple
- ✦ **Nuthatch:** butternut, hickory, spruce
- ✦ **Pine siskin:** birch, eastern hemlock, spruce
- ✦ **Purple finch:** balsam fir, maple
- ✦ **Robin:** white pine, red cedar, crab apple, mountain ash
- ✦ **Sapsucker:** flowering dogwood
- ✦ **Thrush:** chokecherry, flowering dogwood

To attract butterflies, concentrate on plants with long blooming cycles, such as hollyhocks, coneflowers, nasturtiums, sunflowers, and even blossoming weeds. Blooming herbs are a special treat, as irresistible to butterflies as apple pie is to humans. Plants particularly irresistible to various species of butterfly are:

- ✦ **The aster and daisy family,** including asters, dandelions, marigolds, sunflowers, and zinnias
- ✦ **The legume family,** including peas, clover, and lupine

- **The mint family,** including mint, lavender, basil, rosemary, and oregano
- **The parsley family,** including parsley, dill, carrot, fennel, and Queen Anne's lace
- **The violet family,** including violets, pansies, and violas

Offer water in a birdbath,

which has all the features birds want—it is elevated to discourage predators, it offers good footing, its slope is gradual, and it is shallow (birds shun water that is more than a few inches deep). You can add to the attraction by keeping the water fresh and scrupulously free of dirt, leaves, and algae. Butterflies like fresh water too, but will not wade as birds do. A few large stones added to the bath, with flat surfaces that protrude just above the water, offer butterflies a perch to drink from and a sunny place to rest and warm their bodies.

Butterflies, hummingbirds, and most songbirds prefer

brush or mixed woodlands, while wide stretches of clipped grass attract starlings, grackles, pigeons, and other species that compete with songbirds. Consider interrupting those broad sweeps of green with more trees, flower beds, border hedges, and shrubs. Small trees—especially fruit-bearing varieties—and evergreens are good choices, as neither will bury your lawn in shade.

The greater variety of plants

your yard harbors, the greater your chances are of maintaining year-round appeal. Evergreens may go unnoticed in spring and summer, but in winter the shelter and berries they provide will keep visitors interested. In addition to plants that flourish in different seasons, choose plants that create different levels and different mini-habitats. If possible, offer some woods-like patches, some sunny open areas, and some meadow-like border areas between.

Birds and butterflies are attracted to bright colors, so

make sure your yard has plenty of bold splashes throughout. Red is a favorite with both species, and hummingbirds are especially drawn to red, pink, and orange

BRING IN THE BIRDS

I've often wished I had a patent on those hummingbird feeders you buy in garden stores and fill with nectar. It would be a good business to be in. Most people I know are fascinated by hummingbirds, and most have bought a feeder at one time or another. The sales must be staggering. Unfortunately, the tiny, jewel-like creatures don't find the feeders nearly as promising as we do, and sightings can be few and far between. To improve your chances, try planting natural sources of nectar from these sources.

→ Trees and shrubs such as azalea, buddleia, cape honeysuckle, flowering quince, mimosa, and Turk's cap

→ Vines such as cypress, coral honeysuckle, morning glory, and trumpet creeper

→ Flowers such as geraniums, bee balm, wild bergamot, cardinal flower, columbine, coral bells, firespike, four o'clocks, foxglove, fuschia, hosta, impatiens, lupine, prairie blazingstar, petunia, and yucca

tubular flowers. In addition to reds and oranges, butterflies will be drawn by blues, purples, and whites.

Give them shelter. Both birds and butterflies need respite from the weather and a safe place to rest. Birds enjoy shady, secluded branches, well away from noise and predators, and smaller birds will often nest in arbors. Butterflies especially look for shelter from the wind, so plant flowers attractive to them in a sunny, protected spot next to a vine-covered fence, a wall, or a windbreak of shrubs or trees.

Be patient. Remember that you're trying to do something that's very difficult: attract wild animals into a habitat that is to them unfamiliar, unnatural, and possibly hazardous. It may take several seasons and a good deal of experimenting to coax them to you, but the ultimate reward is well worth the effort.

Butterflies and birds flock to brightly colored flower gardens such as this one.

NATURAL PEST CONTROL

It turns out there are all sorts of products most of have in our own kitchens and pantries that are a pest's sign to get up and run. Most of them are pretty effective but not as long-lasting as chemical preparations, so reapplication is needed. On the upside, you won't have to worry about the kids, cats, and dogs getting sick or what the runoff is doing to the groundwater, and you won't be inadvertently

killing beneficial insects like ladybugs, so it's a pretty good trade.

In addition to taking action against specific pests, a few general rules can help you gain control. First, use yellow bulbs in porch and outdoor lights—they don't attract bugs. Another is to bring in insect-eating species such as frogs, toads, lizards, and nonpoisonous snakes (black snakes are especially effective bug-eaters).

✦ Ants: Plant borders act as barriers to ants. Plants that repel them include spearmint, peppermint, and pennyroyal.

✦ Aphids: Nitrogen fertilizers produce just the kind of fast-growing tender shoots that aphids love. Switch to a slow-release fertilizer, settle for a natural growth rate, and you won't attract nearly as many of them. Any that do show up can be discouraged by planting spearmint, peppermint, or pennyroyal near the plants you want to protect. Aphids dislike these and will be discouraged from carrying out their raids.

✦ Deer: This idea literally stinks, and most of us would never consider it for any other critter. But deer are so pervasively destructive, and so impervious to most home remedies, it's worth the unpleasantness. Mix two raw eggs and put them in a clean, empty spray bottle. Fill the bottle with water and leave it in the sun for an afternoon. Spray whatever the deer are eating—they won't like the smell any better than you do, and will move on.

+ **Flies:** Include lots of basil and mint in your garden to keep common flies away.

+ **Mice:** The best mouse repellent I've found is well-used cat litter—the stronger the urine smell, the more effective (I've actually found dead mice in the open bag I've left in the garage). Mice also dislike the smell of peppermint, so sprinkling some pure, strong extract around their haunts will drive them away.

+ **Mosquitoes:** Plant marigolds around the yard and keep several pots on the deck and picnic table—mosquitoes can't stand the smell. If you have a birdbath, it's an ideal spot for mosquitoes to lay their eggs. You can keep this from happening by pouring a few drops of salad oil onto the water. It makes a film that keeps off the insects, and won't harm or interfere with the birds at all.

+ **Slugs and snails:** Because they're closely related, what repels one will usually repel the other, but are not always equally effectively, so experiment. Both slugs and snails hate ashes, so save your winter fireplace sweepings to use in your garden come spring. If you don't have a source of ashes, befriend a woodworker—they don't like sawdust either. If you don't have ashes or sawdust, use beer: press a jar lid upside down into the soil so that the lip is even with the ground, fill with stale beer, and give them a pleasant farewell. The beer loses its appeal about day three, so you'll have to replenish it. In between, remove the soldiers. Neither likes copper, so mounting copper stripping (two inches or wider) around flower beds will keep them out.

+ **Squirrels:** If squirrels keep grabbing the goodies in your pole-mounted bird feeder, buy a length of PVC that's four to five inches in diameter and slide it over the pole. The squirrels won't be able to get a grip on it, won't be able to climb, and only their pride will be the worse for wear.

A Greener Life

It's the twenty-first century. Do you know where your energy dollars are? Living greener isn't a punishment, nor is it a fad. It's the smart thing to do, and no matter who you are or where you live, you can find as many reasons to go green as there are ways to do it.

Line-drying your clothes, in addition to the reasons outlined on pages 104–105, is a great way to lower your utility bills.

GREEN AT HOME

You don't need to do a major home renovation to be more energy efficient. There are some remarkably small, simple steps you can take right now that will make a big difference in the resources your household consumes.

Heating and cooling your home are where most of your energy dollars go. A good place to start saving is to keep a lid on the thermostat. Depending on the weather, every degree above 68°F increases your overall fuel consumption by as much as 3 percent.

If you have forced-air heating, check the ducts to make sure the seams and joints are tight, and that heated air isn't leaking away before it gets to the room you're trying to heat.

Say the word "insulation" and people immediately envision a major league renovation. But some of the most energy-saving steps you can take are definitely minor. You can cut heating bills significantly simply by wrapping hot air ducts and water pipes that pass through unheated parts of the house (like the basement) with insulation. You might need some guidance getting the type that's best suited to the job, but once you've made the purchase, you can install it yourself without much trouble.

Install a programmable thermostat or get into the habit of lowering the heat before bed. Cutting back by ten degrees overnight in winter, and raising it by ten degrees in the summer could also cut your annual fuel bill by as much 20 percent.

Don't try to conserve by using a space heater in one room and turning the rest of the house into an Arctic zone. You don't want the rest of your house to get too cold, and electric space heaters use the most expensive form of fuel there is. Moreover, they're dangerous, and account for more home fires than any other single appliance.

IF YOU DON'T HAVE A PROGRAMMABLE THERMOSTAT AND PLAN TO BUY ONE, CALL YOUR ENERGY PROVIDER FIRST. MANY UTILITIES ARE NOW OFFERING THEM FREE TO CUSTOMERS.

Use your windows to help control the temperature indoors. If your
windows are well-insulated, take advantage of them—keep curtains open
on sunny winter days to get the benefit of the sun's heat. In summer months,
lower the shades on all but north-facing windows during the day.

Building a fire in the fireplace is a cozy way to warm up on a brisk winter day.

WHEN THE WEATHER GETS COOL, REMOVE WINDOW AIR CONDITIONERS OR, IF THEY'RE NOT REMOVABLE, ENCLOSE THEM WITH COVERS.

Close registers and doors in rooms that go unused for long periods in both winter and summer.

Make sure that drapes, sofas, and bookshelves don't block radiators, baseboard heaters, or registers. If you have no choice but to position a piece of furniture in front of a register, close it off.

Use a humidifier in the winter months. Cold and furnace heat dry the air, but returning it to normal levels will make the house feel warmer without raising the temperature.

Have a professional do an annual maintenance check of your furnace. Whatever the cost, you'll recoup it in higher performance. Take care of minor maintenance yourself, such as cleaning or replacing filters regularly and making sure registers are free of dust.

Check for air leaks around windows, baseboards, electrical outlet and switch plates, wall-mounted air conditioners, and openings that accommodate pipes, wiring, and vents coming into the house. Seal up the leaks with caulk or weather stripping.

If you have central air conditioning, make checking the condenser part of your regular lawn care routine. Keep the unit's fins and coils clean, removing grass and leaves as they collect.

In summer months, keep rooms at 78°F or warmer. Below 78 degrees, energy consumption begins to skyrocket, and can increase fuel use by 40 percent.

Before you turn on the air conditioner, try fans. They use far less energy, and in the early months of summer, before heat and humidity become intense, they're often enough to keep you comfortable. Experiment with creating cross-ventilation currents that draw cool air through the house by positioning fans in windows to expel hot air. This is especially effective at night, when the outside temperature is lower than the inside. And wouldn't you rather enjoy the summer scents of mown grass and blossoming flowers instead of sealing yourself in?

A fan is especially effective if you have an attic. A whole-house fan specially designed for this purpose will pull cool air in and send heated air up and out though the roof vents. The attic will act as a cooled cushion protecting the whole house.

You can also cut energy use by alternating air conditioning with fans. After you turn the unit off, the house will stay considerably cool for several hours, and fans will keep the air from feeling stagnant.

If it's time for a new roof, go pale. A light-colored roof reflects sunlight and will keep your house cooler in the summer.

In warm weather, run heat-producing appliances such as the washer, dryer, and dishwasher early in the morning or late at night when the house is cooler and can disperse the heat. In cool weather, use these appliances in the late afternoon and evening, when people are home from work and school and can make use of the extra warmth.

In warm summer months, keep the door to the laundry room closed to avoid adding heat and humidity to the house. In the winter, keep the door open

and, after the dryer is finished, leave the dryer door open as well. Every bit of warmth reduces your furnace's work.

DRESS YOUR WATER HEATER IN INSULATED WRAP. IT'S AN EASY AND INEXPENSIVE DO-IT-YOURSELF PROJECT THAT WILL RESULT IN ENERGY SAVINGS, ESPECIALLY DURING THE WINTER MONTHS.

When it's time for a new washer, consider a front loader.
These models use less water the top loaders, and are usually more efficient
in the spin cycle, meaning you'll run the dryer less.

Stop power leaks. If you think your home electronics are turned off, think again. Most—including televisions, CD and DVD players, DVRs, and almost anything else that operates by remote control, as well as computer peripherals such as monitors, scanners, printers, camera bays, routers, hubs, and external drives—aren't really off, they're in stand-by mode. Energy experts estimate that, in a typical modern home, 5 to 15 percent of the electricity used goes to this kind of seepage. At the very least, unplug all these gadgets before leaving home for a vacation. You might also consider plugging several electronics—such as those in your entertainment center—into a single power bar, and turning it off before you go to bed at night.

Most people set the temperature on their hot water heaters higher than need be. Simply lowering it from 130°F to 120°F will result in noticeable savings. In the summer, when people want cooler showers and baths, you may be able to lower the setting even further. Experiment with lowering the setting until you find the lowest temperature that works for you. Even a few degrees will add up to an energy savings large enough to see on your electric bill.

If your water heater is more than ten years old, it may be operating at less than 50 percent efficiency, even if it delivers all the hot water you need. It might make more economic sense to replace it than to wait for it to wear out. If you do decide to replace it, see if an on-demand water heater makes sense for you, as they use less energy than conventional types.

A drippy faucet is more than just annoying—it's a major source of wasted water and higher water bills. That little kerplunk, kerplunk, kerplunk can go through twenty gallons of water a day— over 7,000 gallons a year. Check all the faucets in your house and take care of any problems. Usually, the solution is no more than replacing the washer.

Check the toilets. The quiet murmur you often here may be the sound of water continuously draining from the tank into the bowl and sending as much as 200 gallons a day straight into the sewer system. To see if your fixture is doing this, sprinkle a few drops of food coloring in the tank. If it shows up in the bowl in the next ten minutes or so, you've got a problem.

The Internet is a formidable research tool. When it's time to buy a new appliance, use it to research the most energy efficient models available. Even if an old appliance isn't quite worn out, you may find that replacing it with a new, more efficient model is more economical to run, so do your homework.

If you have a choice of purchasing a gas dryer or an electric dryer, opt for the gas dryer. There are much less expensive to run than electric dryers.

Do a thorough lighting check of the entire house. Make note of where you can switch to more energy-efficient or lower-wattage bulbs. Dimmers and motion-sensing nightlights are great ways to save energy, especially in rooms like the bathroom and kitchen.

When choosing lamps and light fixtures and planning the lighting in your house, remember that where bright light is needed, one higher-watt bulb is more efficient than several smaller, lower-watt ones. A single 100-watt will cost less to operate and produce more light than three 60-watt bulbs, and one 60-watt bulb will outperform three 40-watt ones.

- -

IN THE CAR

- -

Using less gas makes sense for sense for the environment as well as the family bank account. Here are some steps you can take right now to drive more efficiently.

When miles per hour increase, miles per gallon decrease. Peak operating efficiency for most cars (including hybrids) is in the 30 to 55 mph range, with gas use steadily increasing at higher speeds. Above 55 mph, each additional 10 mph will burn about 15 percent more gas.

Clean house. Lots of us have items we don't really need in our cars. Old books we mean to donate. Tool boxes with enough gear to repair the Titanic. Last summer's picnic hamper, soft drinks and bottles still inside. Sports equipment and sleeping bags and even firewood that has yet to be unloaded. For every 100 pounds of weight you carry, your engine uses an extra 1 to 2 percent of fuel. The figure may sound inconsequential but it all adds up, so clear out the clutter periodically.

Know your PSI. PSI stands for pounds per square inch, the standard for measuring air pressure inside a tire. In addition to the tire's maximum PSI (stamped on the tire wall), which you don't want to aim for, there's a recommended PSI (found in the owner's manual as well as somewhere on the car itself), which you do want to maintain. When air pressure falls below the recommended PSI, the engine has to work harder, so it pays to know your PSI. Checking isn't hard to do, but you may want to buy your own gauge to use at home, since you can only get an accurate reading when the tires haven't been driven for three hours or more.

EVERYONE CAN MAKE A DIFFERENCE
BY MAKING SMALL CHANGES,
WHETHER ITS SOMETHING AS SIMPLE
AS BIKING RATHER THAN DRIVING
OR AS PLEASURABLE AS REUSING
SOMETHING OLD IN A NEW WAY.

Don't idle. Everyone knows that idling sends pollutants into the air, but lot of us feel it's more efficient than turning the car off and on in the space of a few minutes. In most cases, this isn't true. If you're going to idle for more than ten to fifteen seconds, it's actually less polluting to turn the car off and restart it.

Don't floor it. Sudden, all-out accelerations and abrupt stops are hard on your car and burn fuel unnecessarily, so keep a light foot on the accelerator and get into the habit of braking gradually. Hybrids require a slightly different approach, so consult your owner's manual to learn what driving style is most efficient for your vehicle.

Use the AC wisely. Because running the air conditioning takes extra fuel, it makes sense to park in the shade on a sunny day, or shield your windows with a sun deflector. If the day isn't too warm, running the fan and opening the vents may keep you comfortable.

Before you get in the car, consider the alternative. During World War II people were encouraged to ask themselves, "Is this trip necessary?" Today, a good question to ask is "Is this car trip necessary?" There's nothing wrong with biking to the library, or walking a few blocks to a friend's house. In addition to conserving fuel and getting some exercise, it's a chance to feel the sun on your face, notice things in your neighborhood you may not have noticed before, and have an experience that isn't part of your ordinary routine.

REUSE AND REPURPOSE: THE NINE LIVES OF EVERYDAY OBJECTS

There's something satisfying about getting that little bit of extra use out of something. Our grandparents and great-grandparents did it as a matter of necessity, and along with the flour sack dishtowels and re-caned

chairs we inherited their sense of thrift, industry, and independence. Finding new uses for old items seems more challenging today, in a world designed to be disposable, but there are still ways to get the most out of items that would otherwise get tossed.

Don't throw out old placemats

when they no longer suit your china or your decor. Cloth and vinyl placemats can be used to line picnic baskets, dresser drawers, and even silverware drawers, or cut in half and used as padding between delicate china plates. If the mats are cloth, sew two together, leaving one of the short sides free, roll the top edge down and stitch in place over a ribbon drawstring, and you have a mini laundry bag for your next trip out of town, just the right size for soiled lingerie. Two old placements will also make a perfect set of shoe bags. Fold each in half, bringing the short sides together, stitch along the bottom and sides, add a drawstring at the top edge, and your expensive shoes will be protected from dust and accidental scuffing. Quilted placemats are a special prize, as they make perfect potholders. Trim to the desired size and cover raw edges with seam binding. Cut the seam binding three inches longer than needed to make a loop at the finishing corner.

Before you scrap your old range,

save the burners. Scrub them well, scraping off any carbon buildup, and keep them in the garage. They're great for draining potted plants that have just been watered, and make perfect trivets for the picnic table. If you really want to go colorful, give them a few coats of high-gloss spray paint. Or, for a rustic garden look, try a faux verdigris finish.

Instead of tossing last year's Yellow Pages

in the trash, toss them in your car. You never know when you'll need a map or an emergency tow.

Oh, those little slivers of soap.

It's probably the number one thing people try to save, trying everything from melting and pouring into a new mold to melting with a bit of water to make liquid soap. While both of these work, I've always found them a bit too fussy. My method was to make a small drawstring bag of nylon netting, put the slivers inside, and use it as a mini-loofah. Those were the old days. Enter the best friend soap slivers ever had—the small, pretty, inexpensive, and available-

{ In addition to its green appeal, the reuse of old objects, such as these door handles, can add great architectural touches to your home. }

Flea market chairs and china cabinets find
a second home in this living room.

AN OLD TIE RACK MAKES GREAT UNDER-
THE-SINK STORAGE FOR DISH CLOTHS,
TOWELS, SPONGES AND OTHER ITEMS.
NOT ONLY ARE THEY OUT OF SIGHT,
BUT THE CIRCULATING AIR ALLOWS
THEM TO DRY RATHER THAN MILDEW.

at-any-party-store organza gift bag, drawstrings included. Now I buy them in luscious shades that coordinate with my towels.

Plastic bags from the grocery store are great for lining waste baskets. The lighter-weight, almost papery ones are ideal for storing baguettes and artisan bread in, as they keep it from drying without smothering it so much the crust goes soft and tough.

Old toothbrushes, cleaned and sterilized, are right at the top of my can't-do-without list. Use them to clean anything small and intricate, from jewelry to bicycle chains to graters and the garlic press. They're great for brushing dust, crumbs, and pet hairs from the computer keyboard, scouring the grout between tiles, and dozens of other small-scale cleaning jobs.

If you see an old vinyl shower curtain at a garage sale, grab it. It will make a great painting drop cloth, waterproof ground covering when you're camping out, protective covering for firewood and outdoor furniture or, come winter, a windshield blanket that will keep frost from building up on both front and back car windows. To make the windshield blanket, cut a piece slightly larger than the window and glue magnets along the upper and lower edges to hold it in place.

Tired of your crafts and fine art brushes getting their bristles bent? Or tipping over and spilling? Dust all the salt and crumbs from a Pringles canister and store them there. Even if it gets tipped over, the lid will keep them from scattering.

Empty egg cartons are great for storing jewelry, office supplies, and other small items. They make perfect trays when you're working on a craft project with small pieces—such as beads, embellishments, or sequins—that you want to keep separate. And every home workshop should have one for screws, washers, and small nails, which will be even less likely to get mixed up if you glue a small magnet to the bottom of each cup.

No room in the linen closet? Store extra blankets in your empty

A vintage basket serves as a flower pot with a kitsch flair.

luggage. Tuck a used dryer sheet in as well and both your blankets and your luggage will smell fresh when it's time for use.

My mother never bought wrapping paper. She bought tissue paper and kept a box of last year's cards, along with glue, glitter, and ribbon, and left the decorating to us. Watching someone unwrap a gift decorated especially for them is one of my favorite holiday memories. The only wrapping paper I buy is the cheapest, ugliest paper there is when it's on sale—then I turn it over and use the blank side. The card box is also my source for gift tags, place cards, matting for small pictures, as well as scraps for paper mosaics and collage.

Old clean T-shirts make excellent soft clothes for polishing delicate glassware and silver, and anything else that needs

DRYER SHEETS:
THE INDISPENSABLE DISPOSABLE

Isn't it ironic that something designed to use once and throw away would have more lives than a cat? Dryer sheets came on the market way back in the 1970s, and people have delighted in finding second uses for them ever since. Below, the best uses for spent dryer sheets:

↣ When sewing thread tangles, running the sheet over it will cut down on snarls.

↣ They wipe up fine, dry spills such as talcum powder and flour more efficiently than a paper towel or damp cloth can.

↣ A used sheet makes a great dust cloth—especially for television screens, where static and dust combine.

↣ Wipe window blinds with a used sheet and the blinds will stay dust free longer.

↣ Since used sheets retain their scent after use, use one wherever you want light freshening. Tuck them into gym bags and linen closets, slide them under the litter box and floor mats of the car, or cut them into pieces and place between the pages of books that have begun to smell a bit musty.

↣ Wrap a dry sheet around your hand and use it to brush pet hair from clothes and furniture.

↣ Not all living creatures love that subtle fresh scent. It repels mice, and stuffing used sheets into crevices they might use as entry points will keep you from hearing those disturbing, tell-tale rustlings in the middle of the night.

↣ If you plan on spending time outdoors, tuck one in a pocket or tie one to a belt loop—mosquitoes and other summertime pests will leave you alone.

↣ When you just don't feel like scrubbing the pan with the baked-on food, add a used dryer sheet, fill with water, and your job will be easier in the morning.

A CHANDELIER RESCUED FROM THE LANDFILL CAN STILL BE GREEN WHEN IT IS OUTFITTED WITH CFLS.

a soft touch. Wrap one around the head of a mop or broom and use to sweep dust and cobwebs from high corners and gently dust ceiling fixtures.

Old, dull steak knives belong in the kitchen junk drawer as well as every pencil cup in the house. They're useful for all sorts of tasks, including slicing through packing tape, digging melted wax out of candle holders, and popping keys off the computer keyboard to clean underneath. They're sharp enough to get the job done yet dull enough to avoid cuts and accidental damage.

Long before there were expensive pet toys, there were old socks. Knotted into lengths or loops, they're perfect for chew toys and tug-of-war ropes for dogs. For cats, knot a scoop of catnip into the toe and even the most aloof cat becomes a kitten under the influence. To your pets, these inexpensive toys have an added benefit—they're comforting because they're yours. Even if the socks are well washed, they still have the familiar smell of home.

If you burn scented candles, save the wax that's left when the wick has burned away. Punch holes in an envelope, then seal the bits inside or place several chunks in a sachet bag and use to scent your drawers. Or re-melt the wax to make new candles. If you don't have enough of one color for a whole candle, combine colors that go together, pouring one layer and letting it cool before adding the next. Since the process of melting wax can be dangerous, be sure to find how-to instructions for safe handling.

INDEX

PHOTOGRAPHY CREDITS

Pages 2 - 3: Wendell T. Webber; Page 5: Mark Lohman; Page 6 (from left): Beatriz Da Costa, Tria Giovan; Page 7 (from left), 164: Robin Stubbert, Keith Scott Morton; Page 10: Robin Stubbert; Page 13 - 16: Keith Scott Morton; Page 18: Steven Randazzo; Page 20: Keith Scott Morton; Page 21: Susie Cushner; Page 23: Beatriz Da Costa; Page 25: Lucas Allen; Page 26: Janis Nicolay; Page 29: Keith Scott Morton; Page 30: Frances Janisch; Page 33: Lara Robby/Studio D; Page 35: David Prince; Page 37: Frances Hammond; Page 38: Tria Giovan; Page 39: Wendell T. Webber; Page 40: Keith Scott Morton; Page 43: Andrew McCaul; Page 44: Karyn Millet; Page 47: Eric Roth; Page 48: Laura Moss; Page 50: David Lewis Taylor; Pages 51 - 52: Ellen McDermott; Page 54: Wrangler Home's Bar Harbor Curio Cabinet in Albermarle Brown; Page 55: Maura Daniel Couture Lighting's Mimi Gold Chandelier; Page 57: Janis Nicolay; Page 58: Robin Stubbert; Page 61: Frances Janisch; Page 62: Robin Stubbert; Page 65: Don Freeman; Page 66: Aimee Herring; Page 68: Keith Scott Morton; Page 71: Country Living and Carpet One Floor & Home; Page 72: Keith Scott Morton; Page 73: Anastassios Mentis; Page 75: Keller + Keller; Page 77: Mark Lunde/Getty Images; Pages 78 - 81: Keith Scott Morton; Page 82: Janis Nicolay; Page 84: Gridley & Graves; Page 87: Keith Scott Morton; Page 88: Joseph De Leo; Page 91: Keller + Keller; Page 92: Keith Scott Morton; Page 95: ML Harris/Getty Images; Page 96: Wendell Weber; Page 98: Keith Scott Morton; Page 99: Steven Randazzo; Pages 100 - 101: Keith Scott Morton; Page 103: Tria Giovan; Page 105: Susie Cushner; Page 107: Keith Scott Morton; Page 108: Creative Containers' Black and White Damask Ironing Board Cover; Page 110: Lucas Allen; Page 113: Ellie Miller; Page 114: Robin Stubbert; Page 117: Ellen McDermott; Page 118: Ray Kachatorian; Page 119: Lara Robby/Studio D; Page 121: Lodge's Pre-Seasoned Cast-Iron skillet; Page 123: Robin Stubbert; Page 124: Laura Moss; Page 125: Wendell T. Webber; Page 126: Keller + Keller; Page 128: Jane Armstrong/Jupiter Images; Page 130: Beatriz Da Costa; Page 133: Andrew McCaul; Page 134: Justin Bernhaut; Page 136: Lucas Allen; Page 139: Burcu Avsar; Page 140: Steven Randazzo; Page 142: Robin Stubbert; Page 144: Ann Stratton; Page 145: iStockphoto; Page 146: Steven Randazzo; Page 148: Richard Young/Foodpix/Jupiter Images; Page 150: Debra McClinton ; Page 152: Beatriz Da Costa; Page 153: Charles Schiller; Page 155: Robin Stubbert; Page 157: Anastassios Mentis; Page 158: Alan Richardson; Page 160: Susie Cushner; Pages 161 - 163: Charles Schiller; Page 164: Ellen McDermott; Page 167: Gridley & Graves; Page 168: Wendell T. Webber; Page 170: Charles Schiller; Page 172: John Granen; Page 174:; Kathryn Kleinman/Jupiter Images; Page 177: Mark Lohman; Page 178: Colin McGuire; Page 179: Robin Stubbert; Page 180: William Steele; Page 182: Andrew Drake; Pages 184 -185: Brooke Slezak; Page 186: Robin Stubbert; Page 187: Charles Schiller/Jupiter Images; Page 188: Andre Baranowski; Pages 189 - 190: iStockphoto; Page 191: André Baranowski; Page 192: Marion Brenner/Jupiter Images; Page 193: Allison Miksch/Jupiter Images; Page 194: Ryan Benyi; Page 196: Andrew Drake; Page 198: Ann Stratton; Page 200: J Muckle/Studio D; Page 201: Aimee Herring; Pages 203 - 208: Keith Scott Morton; Page 212: Laura Moss; Page 214: Robin Stubbert; Page 217: Kindra Clineff; Pages 218 - 220: Keith Scott Morton